DATE DUE

NOV 2 6 2004	
DEC 2 2 2004	
MAY 2 6 2005	
DEC 2 3 2005	
3.8.06	
JUN 1 5 2006	

GAYLORD   PRINTED IN U.S.A.

Horses
Behavin' Badly

Horses
Behavin' Badly

Training Solutions
for Problem Behaviors

Dr. Jim and Lynda McCall

Half Halt Press, Inc.

Boonsboro, Maryland

Horses Behavin' Badly
Training Solutions for Problem Behaviors

Published in the United States of America by
Half Halt Press, Inc.
P.O. Box 67
Boonsboro, MD 21713

Photographs by Lynda McCall
Jacket design by Design Point, Inc.
Front jacket photo by Helen Peppe

Horses Behavin' Badly is intended for educational purposes, to help the reader understand horses better. However, no book — this one included — can possibly cover every possible response. Horses are, after all, individuals. Accordingly, neither the authors nor the publisher have liability or responsibility for any actions arising from the information shared in this book.

Library of Congress Cataloging-in-Publication Data

McCall, Jim, 1943—
    Horses behavin' badly : training solutions for problem behaviors / Jim and Lynda McCall.
       p.   cm.
       ISBN 0-939481-50-2
         1. Horses——Behavior. 2. Horses——Training
I. McCall, Lynda.   636.1
II. Title.   MCC
               5.04
SF281.M34 1997
636.1'08'35——dc21   97—41021
                                  CIP

Contents

Introduction

" There is nothing better for the inside of a man than the outside of a horse."

Will Rogers, among others

Our daily life revolves around horses. Our house is surrounded by barns and fields full of horses. We get up in the morning thinking about horses and end our day talking about what we learned. Horses are our neighbors, our teachers, and our pupils.

We have spent our lives trying to understand them. In doing so, we have learned about ourselves. Horses are mirrors that reflect our strengths and weaknesses. They have taught us universal truths, showed the meaning of true courage, and shared with us their uniqueness.

Every horse we have met has been a unique individual. Each of them has had its own personality with specific needs and wants. Yet, the one thing we have found that all horses have in common is that they strive to find harmony. Harmony within the herd, where a horse's position in the herd reflects his inherent dominance. Harmony within the environment, as it is driven by the cyclical nature of the seasons, the natural movements of the herd, and the routines of human control.

The root of the problems in 'horses behavin' badly' is an inability of the horse to find harmony — harmony with his man-made environment, harmony in his contact with humans. Horses, like children, think they want to be the boss, to control the situation, but, actually, they long to be told what to do. Being dominated provides security, as long as the horse trusts the human to make wise decisions.

We hope this book will help you to understand the horse better. We hope it will make you "horse-wise," that is, to widen the channel of communication between two species whose destinies have been intertwined. If you want to find that magical union that can exist between horse and man for yourself, you must stop and take the time to search for understanding. But the rewards will be one of your greatest gifts. It has been so for us.

Jim and Lynda
Mt. Holly, Arkansas

CHAPTER 1

Expressions:
The Language of the Horse

. . . ears perked, eyes focused, neck extended, bringing the head to the closest safe distance from the unknown object, the body alive with energy and muscle tone, a heightened state of mental awareness (curiosity)

. . . a generalized dull attitude, ears half-turned and flopped sideways, droopy eye lids, lack of muscle tone, sloppy stride, a step from being asleep (boredom)

. . . eyes wide open, ears perked, neck arched high, perching head at peak height, legs up under body poised for movement in any direction, extreme muscle tension, an explosion waiting to happen (terror)

The twitch of an ear, the curl of a lip, a tightness around the eye, tension through the body. . . these expressions are the "words" the horse uses to communicate. His world, the equine community, is well-schooled in the language of expression. The absence of sound is not a sign of silence. The members of the herd carry on subtle conversations. A boss mare cocks her head and flattens an ear as a young filly gets too close to her territory. In reply, the youngster tucks her tail and moves away, perhaps expressing her displeasure with a wrinkled nose about the way the power structure does things — not unlike the youth of today. On the outskirts of the band, the young are engaged in boisterous discussions. Contests about who can run the fastest or turn the quickest are constant. Bossy colts pick on fillies. Fillies dance and prance around. The dialogue is endless.

Learning to read the language of the horse gives insight into the way horses feel — how they relate to their world and, more importantly, how they perceive us. By understanding how a horse feels, it is possible to manipulate that horse into being the kind of individual that horse stories are told about: the horse that carried his rider at top speed till he died of exhaustion; the horse that stood over his rider, shading the fallen cowboy for two days in the blazing sun till he was spotted from the air by a helicopter. For these horses, their first commitment was to please their rider. For these riders, their first commitment was to ride as one with a horse.

In order for you to achieve this union, you must first understand the language of the horse. Learning to recognize the basic expressions is like learning to speak a new language, but this language is not Russian, Greek or Sanskrit. It is not completely foreign or, seemingly, incomprehensible. The language of expression is a universal language which transcends the kingdom of mammals. There are expressions, common among species, that don't need translation. A dog with his ears pinned and teeth bared looks very similar to the look of a stallion before his charge. Indeed, this visual display is not too different from two guys bowed up and ready to get into a knockdown dragged out fight. In all instances, the communication indicates "BEWARE! I am ready to take you on!"

This is an obvious example, but the language of expression is a subtle part of our own human development. Unfortunately, the use of verbal sounds has made us lazy. We rely upon words to transmit meaning and feelings. Words can lie. Expressions cannot. So let's take a step backward to our primordial past as we try to relate to the language of the horse and enter a world where expressions communicate feelings — a world where dominance with power and understanding reigns. Then, the mythical Centaur, a creature half-man, half-horse will live again.

The language of the horse is based upon six basic feelings which can be identified in the foal very shortly after birth: *Peaceful, Curious, Submissive, Spirited, Confidence,* and *Desire.* Each one of these building blocks of the equine language has a paired, opposite state. For example, a foal cannot be peaceful when he is angry. Together, we now have twelve basic "words" to help understand how the horse relates to his environment.

Peaceful and *Angry*
Curious and *Perceptive*
Submissive and *Aggressive*
Spirited and *Depressed*
Confidence and *Fear*
Desire and *Content*

For us, these words may be adjectives, nouns, verbs, or adverbs but for the horse, these expressions modify actions. They describe how he feels about running, trotting, jumping, resting, or everything else he does. A single word to describe a single feeling? How we wish it were so. Each of the feelings can be expressed in varying intensities. It is possible to be a little curious or a lot curious or anything in between. Unfortunately, our English lanuage

3

doesn't have ten to fifty words for various feelings of differing intensities of curious, so we are locked into saying "That horse is sure curious about that." It is the feel that you have about horses that will tell you *how curious* — and *how curious* is very important.

Suppose the young horse you are riding is mildly curious about a piece of black plastic laying on the ground. Chances are he will walk right up to it, smell it and ride off nice and easy. On the other hand, if your colt is extremely curious about the plastic, he will probably blow out his nose, stiffen his front legs as he tenses up and gets ready to run off. The intensity of the feeling dictates the most probable action of the horse. Knowing the intensity tells you what your response should be.

Sound complicated? It's not. In fact, it is a beautifully simplistic language. And, contrary to public opinion, you do not have to be one of the gifted few to reap the rewards of speaking with horses. This myth, that only a few people are born with the ability to communicate with horses, has (like most myths) an element of truth to it. Since the beginning of recorded history, stories have been told about people who could do amazing things with horses. In the fourth century B.C., a Greek soldier and historian by the name of Xenophon acknowledged in his treatise on horse training that there were certain individuals that could communicate with horses and train them to do things with miraculous ease. He thought that these people were touched by Pegasus or blessed by a god with the power to impart their will on horses.

Throughout the centuries that followed little was written about these folks, but their talents colored the folklore of the times. A more recent and documented record of a man who could speak with horses occurred in England soon after the turn of the last century. Early in

4

his twenties, this man who came to be known as the Whisperer, was called to the English Court. The Queen, it seems, had a problem with her prized Thoroughbred stallion. He was a rogue. No one could handle him and it was nearly impossible to control him in the breeding shed.

Upon his arrival at the Queen's stud, the Whisperer requested that the stallion be placed in a boarded-up dark stall. As the Whisperer entered the stall, he left instructions for no one to open the door until he knocked. For over an hour, war raged. Then came a knock on the door. Out came the Whisperer with a respectful stallion at the end of his leadshank. From that day forward, the stallion was totally under the control of the Whisperer. No one else. Just the Whisperer.

Yes, a few people are born with an innate ability to communicate with horses just like a few people are born with a gift to compose music like Beethoven, or to paint like Rembrandt. Yet that does not mean that you must have The Gift to be able to talk with horses any more than it means that only gifted people can compose music or create art.

Besides, the key to learning the language of the horse is readily available to all who choose to try. As we mentioned before, expressions are a part of human communication. Granted, they are a smaller part, and unfortunately, a neglected part. To change that, start now to receive information with your eyes are well as your ears. Body language and facial expressions are not simply the tools of actors and actresses. They are an ancient means of communication that transcends language barriers. Fear, joy, love, anger and pain are just some of the expressions that you can recognize in anyone regardless of their race, creed or nationality.

Can it be a big step to learn to recognize the feelings of our noble companion, the horse? For over 5000 years horses have been the companions of man. If man was not in tune with horses, they would still be as wild as their cousin, the zebra.

So stop now and begin listening to your horse. He is ready, willing and able to serve as your tutor. Watch him. He has been talking to you all the time. You may have just been deaf. As you begin, look for the basic things. How does he feel about doing the things you like him to do? Is he content or relaxed? Does he appear to want to please you? Or does he do what you asked because he is afraid you will hurt him if he doesn't? Is he angry or, worse yet, contemptuous of you? Perhaps, even more importantly, how does your horse feel when he does something that you don't want him to do? Is he scared, confused, mad, sour, angry?

A horse is a kaleidoscope of expressions and feelings changing from moment to moment, so speaking "Horse" requires that you are constantly tuned in. At first, your horse may appear to be surprised or perhaps even skeptical at your attempt to understand and communicate in his own language. If your intentions are honorable, this will quickly pass and the conversation will flow. Your horse will try his best to school you in the language of expression. He will devise imaginative ways to get your attention, let you know of his needs and wants, tell you about his aches and pains, and, if you listen very carefully, he will even tell you how to train him to be the best that he can be. These directives are usually communicated through very simple actions. Most horsemen are familiar with the call of their favorite horse acknowledging their appearance (a simple "Hello"). Nickering around feeding time could be translated "Hurry up! I sure am hungry!"

Head tossing and aggressive actions associated with a feeding routine could be a horse's way of telling you that the barn is not being fed according to the laws of an equine herd. You are feeding the submissive horses before the dominant ones. The words might be "Hey, dummy! I'm supposed to eat before that horse!"

These displays are relatively easy to interpret and the more that you acknowledge what your horse is saying, the more it will tell you. One of the most communicative horses we ever had was a tiny little thoroughbred filly that we bred, raised and raced off the farm. She grew up expecting to be listened to and by the time she was four, we were amazed at what she would tell us.

Each morning after she ate her breakfast, we would groom her and check her body for soundness. Any indication of inflammation, no matter how small the swelling or minor the heat, was attended to. Throughout the process, Wish would stand perfectly still as our hands searched her entire body for a hint of soreness. Then one day as the process began, Wish moved. She began to paw with her left leg. Confused, we asked her to quit but she continued. Then she dropped her nose down to her pastern. As we moved round to check the leg, she stopped pawing. An examination revealed a minuscule amount of heat in the back of the ankle. From that day forward, Wish continued to help with her morning exam.

And then she moved into directing her training routine. The day following a race, our standard procedure was to walk the filly until she loosened up. Then she was asked to move into a slow trot. Again, after she loosened up, the trot was extended; if she wasn't experiencing too much body soreness from the race, she was eventually worked up to a slow canter. For about six months, we stood at the rail and told the rider when to move to the next gait. Then Wish took over. It was astonishing. She performed exactly as we had orchestrated. Our instructions to the rider became "Just let her do her own thing." She never overdid it. She never cheated. She worked until she was loosened up, quit and walked back to the barn.

In the pages that follow, we are going to sort out the basic expressions of the horse to help you become more proficient at using and interpreting the language. As you will see, once you speak "Horse," a whole new world opens and you will be well on your way to becoming one with a horse.

CHAPTER 2

Aggression, But Not Anger

. . . skin around the eye drawn tight back, ears laid flat back, nostrils pinched, lips taut, revealing the teeth, body poised for movement (aggression)

. . . a quick movement away, tail tucked, ears turned backwards towards aggressor, fearful eyes, a slouched body (submission)

. . . skin around the eye drawn tight back, ears laid flat back, nostrils pinched and flared, lips taut revealing teeth, body tense but lacking a commitment to attack (anger)

Rose was a quiet girl. She barely ever spoke above a whisper. Her personality matched her to a tee. Small in height, slight in frame, demure by all standards — except one. Rose could dominate a horse like an animal trainer in the circus controls lions and tigers and bears.

One on one with her horse, Rose was master of all. She could ride bareback without a saddle and bridle and her horse would perform all that was asked. Her stature and abilities made her a perfect model for the photographers who came to document our breaking technique known as "Tackless Training."

Rose could ride without a bridle and her horse would perform all that was asked.

Did Rose arrive at college with the gifts of the Whisperer? No! It was a long hard road for Rose to over-come her shy, non-aggressive nature and take mastery of the horse.

Handling aggression is one of the hardest parts of horse training. For many females like Rose, aggression is just a concept. It may be because women are inherently less aggressive or because girls are not usually exposed to the same kind of competitive sports that their male coun-terparts are. We can debate the cause, but the fact is most women do not show aggression without first becoming angry. This is confusing to the horse.

For the horse, these two expressions, aggression and anger, are separate emotions. A horse who gets angry may or may not become aggressive. In other words, a horse can be aggressive without being angry. In fact, about the only time a horse becomes angry is when his aggressive ges-tures are not respected.

The structure of the unit is glued together with the dominant individual aggressively telling lower-ranking horses what to do. Here, Bluebeard, the dominant mare in a band of thirty, tells every other mare to stay away from her feed tub— or to walk the plank! Order in the band is maintained.

To train horses well, we must learn to think like horses especially where it concerns the role of aggression and submission. Aggression is not a bad thing. It is the driving force that holds the herd together. The structure of the unit is glued together with the dominant individual aggressively telling lower ranking horses what to do. Less dominant horses are expected to show submission and obey the wishes of the superiors. This maintains herd harmony. This is the way a horse is most content. He knows who to respect and who he can push around.

To pull a horse out of the herd and place him in a stall does not change the way he thinks about the world. He still expects some critters to be dominant and others to be submissive. A horse thinks that he is dominant over chickens, cats, cows, goats and some dogs.

However, the verdict is still out for some horses

about their relationship to people. Unfortunately, there are horses that are sure they are the aggressors and people are worms. These horses started out, just like every other foal, apprehensive about people. They spent their early lives pondering the order of the universe and their place in it. Their instincts told them to be scared and submissive towards the omnivore known as man. Yet the humans that these horses were exposed to behaved in strange ways. They acted as if they were submissive to him. They jumped back if he turned his tail towards them. If he ran too close, they lunged out of his way, acting as if afraid he was going to run them down.

Basically, foals treated like this see submission and fear from the folks that handle them. It is no wonder that they grow up thinking that horses are supposed to tell humans what to do. So they do. They lead humans around on the leadshank. They only do what is asked if they want to do it anyway. You know the kind. And, hopefully, you know only the "good" kind.

When a horse has this attitude about people, you hope that his basic nature is kind, gentle and easy to get along with. Then he becomes the dominant horse who accepts the responsibility for the humans in his herd. On the other hand, if the horse's basic nature is "Me first at any cost," you are riding a horse whose own wants, needs and wishes are his top priority. You are just along for the ride. If you get there and back in one piece, fine. If you don't, that's also fine. It doesn't matter to him as long as you don't tell him to do much along the way.

His past training only served to convince him that submission to the whims of man only needs to be minimal. He allows himself to be ridden and to accept some direction but, ultimately, he has the right of refusal when he has had enough. And he decides just when that is.

One of the worst horses that ever came to us for training fell into this category. Chika was a two-year-old stud who thought he was King Kong. He didn't look the part: narrow, uncoordinated, plain. A little horse, just over 14 hands and weighing a mere 650 pounds. Oblivious to the dichotomy, Chika believed it was his inalienable right to bite, kick or strike out at any human who got in his way. Was he born like this? No! He was raised by some folks who had never had a horse before and were scared to death of him from the day he was born. They taught him that he was big, bad medicine.

Can you change these horses? Only if it's worth it! Really bad horses like this have a slim chance of ever being transformed into kind, gentle, trustworthy mounts. The key to reshaping their behavior is to convince them that you are more dominant than them. That means, stronger, meaner and, sometimes, even crueler. To rise to the challenge means that you are willing to take the risk that this horse may cripple or kill you.

This is not an overstatement. Chika greeted each person who tried to enter his stall either with a teeth-bared charge or both barrels of his hind feet aimed directly at their chests. Finally, all attempts at a "gentling process" were abandoned and he was roped and taken to a soft area. There he was tied four-footed and thrown to the ground. Once restraint had been achieved, attempts were made to gently touch his body. He responded to all efforts by trying to reach around and grab any part of a human body with his teeth in hopes of ripping flesh.

For several hours the battle continued. Finally, the horse gave up and allowed himself to be touched. In a step-by-step progress, ropes were removed as he continued to accept human touch. At the end of the session he was haltered and standing still, allowing himself to be touched by human hands.

But that wasn't the end of it. During the next twelve weeks of our association with Chika, you could never trust him not to try and nail you if he got the chance. By the end of the summer, Chika accepted the fact that he was broke to ride.

Was it worth it? Not in our opinion. Had the horse not been used for teaching, the risk of getting seriously hurt far outweighed any contribution Chika would ever make to a meaningful horse/human relationship.

Like disease, we believe that the best way to handle this situation is to guard against it. This means that you must gain an understanding about how to become the leader in your herd of two. Your best teacher is the horse himself. Watch how horses relate between themselves. The dominant individual makes the rules.

"I get the first feed tub."

"You must move out of my way."

"I can receive all the attention when I want it."

"I will be put up at night first."

Whatever that horse wants, he gets. He doesn't have to scream and yell all the time. He doesn't have to be continuously attacking. So how does this horse maintain his position of power? Through respect.

The other members of the herd respect this individual's abilities. He may be smarter, quicker, stronger, faster, more self-confident, or any combination of the above. A horse gains a position of dominance over other members of the herd because the horses below him respect him as their leader. He may still have to occasionally use aggression and threaten to bite or kick a horse who is testing the order, but the aggression has direction and meaning and lacks malice or revenge. He delivers his aggressive gesture swiftly upon the perpetrator and holds no grudge for the future. It is the law and order of the equine world.

These traits are important to portray if you are to be the dominant member of your herd. Obviously we can't be stronger or faster, but we can be smarter and not hold grudges. We can understand the things that are important to the horse (things that the horse will respect) and show him that we are capable of being the kind of individual that is worthy of his respect.

You begin by making the rules and living by them. The closer your rules are to the by-laws of the herd, the easier it will be for your horse to understand them. But whatever rules you choose, maintain them — just as the dominant horse would. The crossover rules from horse to man include:

You may not bite, kick, or paw at me.

You may not bump, push or shove me.

When I say move, you must yield.

Failure to comply results in an immediate reprimand. Nothing destroys respect faster than for a horse to find himself being beaten for something he did five minutes or more ago. In fact, this horse has no idea why he is being beaten. He assumes that you are an irrational being. He may learn to hate you or fear you, but he will not respect you.

This is why in the horse world, "If you do the crime, you must pay the price immediately!" The judicial system is also weighted: an eye for an eye, a pat for a pat. The horse who timidly brushes against you as he is distracted probably needs only a brief verbal scolding. The horse who boldly tries to run you over needs the fire knocked out of him. A horse will respect you for understanding his motivations and dealing out the correctly measured punishment for his action. A horse will not respect a trainer who continuously beats him in the same manner regardless of the situation. He will be afraid of him, and fear and respect are worlds apart.

Another way we gain a horse's respect is to be smart enough to teach the horse what we want to do. Then, to be an outstanding teacher, we need to have the ability to know when a horse is giving an all-out effort and when he is just barely trying.

These attributes of great teachers transcend species lines. Just ask your friends whom they respect. Their lists will include people who have influenced their lives in a positive way; someone who took the time to teach them something important in their lives. You can be that person for your horse. He will admire you for your patience, understanding, consistency, perseverance, and willingness to try and communicate with him. But, most importantly, a horse will respect you for your ability to dominate him. This means that you must be able to read his aggressive gestures towards you and know why he feels the way he does.

Recognizing aggressive expressions is the easy part. The ears, the eyes, the position of the chin are obvious signs to his mental state. Why he feels that way is much harder to learn. Begin by looking at what you did. Horses (except stallions and mares with PMS) don't get up on the wrong side of the bed. The odds are that you caused the aggression. Now the important question becomes, "As the dominant leader, did I have the right to act in such a manner?" Unless you were cruel, stupid or inconsistent, the answer is probably "Yes, I did."

His aggression should then be met head on. Swift and just retaliation forms the structure of your benevolent dominance. Compassion, kindness, understanding, and praise are doorways through which you must pass in order to join ranks with Rose in the exclusive club known as the Masters of the Horse.

CHAPTER 3

Riding Over Fear

The two-year-old colt is gentle and started well under saddle. He had a good foundation put on him in the breaking pens and, today, you are going to take him on his first trail ride. Even though he is familiar with the countryside, he looks about as though he is seeing everything for the first time. At the first little stream, the youngster adamantly refuses to put one foot in the shallow water. He balks. He backs up. Under strong urging, he runs sideways. His nostrils flare. The whites of his eyes show. He breaks into a sweat. He wheels around to go back the way he came.

The stream where all this terrified refusal is taking place may be a spot in the pasture where this green colt has crossed on his own a hundred times before. But the saddle and rider on his back seem to have bewitched him into believing that this once familiar little stream is now a crater of doom with molten lava flowing through it.

If you think like a horse, you know the reason why this colt has become petrified about something so familiar. He's afraid of the restraints on him which may not, in his mind, allow him to cross the water without falling or drowning. You see, he has never carried weight over wet footing. He has never been under the control of a halter or bridle while not on solid ground.

To anthropomorphically put his thoughts into words: "I don't trust this human. I'm afraid he will do something that will cause me to lose my balance when the footing gets bad." This belief strikes as much fear into the mind of the horse as someone handcuffing and hobbling you before sending you into a house of horrors.

There are many possible solutions to the problem. You could step down, removing your weight from the horse's back and lead the horse across the creek. You could get assistance from the rear at driving the horse over, or you could convince the horse that your wish for him to cross the water is greater than his desire to resist. Of course, this usually requires whips, spurs, and strength of mind and body — behavior that will cause the horse to become more afraid of you than he is of the obstacle.

In this particular situation, the right choice from the possible solutions depends on two things: how much the horse trusts you and, more importantly, how much the horse trusts himself. With a younger horse, most trainers would be more understanding and try to reduce the fear rather than to resort to bullying and pain to force the colt to go somewhere he feels insecure. Good trainers would rather build a young horse's confidence.

In the case of refusal by an older horse, our patience may be less generous. The first choice is likely to be the bit, whip and spur method. Yet, in many instances, the older horse is also genuinely afraid. The question now becomes "How do we tell for sure whether the animal is showing fear or just saying "Hell, No, I won't go!"

The western artist, Charles Russell, had a real eye for horses showing fear. While all of his paintings captured the soul of horses, some of his most demonstrative examples of honest-to-goodness fear involved scenes of horses meeting up with grizzly bears along the trail. Crossing a ditch or stream may not have the same danger factor as running up on a bear, but the expression is still shown in the same way.

It is not difficult to see how a horse expresses fear:

- the whites of the eye show;
- the ears turn out as the chin is raised;
- the head turns away from the obstacle causing the fear;
- the muscles tense and become hard and rigid.

When a horse shows all these signs, he is not just apprehensive or slightly afraid. He is definitely fearful and the "flight or fight syndrome" is kicking in. This means there is reduced peripheral circulation and the spleen dumps its blood reservoirs; all of which adds up to heightened oxygen transport as reflected in the flared nostrils and the forced respiration. The image is complete as the body is placed into either a flight or fright position.

Now that we can determine whether the fear is real or not, a big dilemma still remains: How do we deal with the horse's fear, especially when there isn't a grizzly? How do we convince our horse that the terror in his mind is not real when he is positive it is?

Recently we received a letter from a friend which explained her solution to a similar problem she was having with her fractious mare. She had been looking for a new place to work her mare.

". . . I headed off in a new direction down the street that led to a seldom used dirt road. Not a good idea! First we took fright at three chickens who were minding their own business. Then we took exception to the yellow stripe down the middle of the street; I had to cross the street to get to the dirt road. We then spooked at three surveyor's flags on a tree

21

branch. Now, keep in mind, it's only, at the max, 300 yards from my little street to the dirt road. Needless to say, I am starting to get a trifle miffed. But, now for the coup de grace. There was a sheet, beige background with pretty pink flowers that had wrapped itself around a small tree. You would have thought we have been attacked by terrorists the way my mare was carrying on. I had to actually get off and kill this faded piece of linen by stomping on it half a dozen times before goof-ball would move past it. Thank the Lord that no one took that moment to drive by or they would have seen the city's only lady lawyer jumping up and down on a piece of bed linen shouting "Is it dead enough for you? Can I stop now?" When all was said and done, it had taken us 15 minutes to go 300 yards."

This approach is one most of us have tried. A horse spies an object that sends an adrenaline surge through his body. You casually look over at the thing and say "Oh, that's nothing to be afraid of" and the horse immediately begins to question *your* sanity.

Clearly, this tells us that horses don't think like people. It is human logic to assume that if we show the horse we are not afraid of the spook, then the horse should not be either. This is what happens instead: we show the horse that we are not afraid of something that he perceives as a horseflesh-eating creature from outer space. The horse becomes convinced that his rider is an oblivious being that is going to be gobbled up by the first such creature to come along. To add insult to injury, the horse is also sure that he is more attuned to survival than his dim-witted rider, and that he had better save himself even if he can't save the fool on his back.

An approach that has a better chance of success in similar situations works like this: the moment you feel (or see) the horse become apprehensive or fearful towards an object, mimic his anxiety by tightening up and intensely focusing on the event or object causing the problem. The horse is now aware that you are not blind and deaf; you have acknowledged the presence of potential danger. Then relax your body and continue to ride on as if you have decided that there was nothing to fear.

This makes "horse sense." Instead of calling the horse stupid for being afraid, you have acknowledged that there was a reason for his concern. But, by using your superior intelligence, you have determined that there is nothing to fear. The situation has been neutralized.

This technique is similar to what happens in the horse world. Two horses are going down a trail and one spots a spook-able object. He tenses up and focuses intently on the object. Immediately, the other horse hones in on the same subject. If one of the horses determines there is nothing to fear, relaxes and proceeds on his journey, the other horse follows his lead and continues on. All this happens within the blink of an eye.

During the early training of a green colt out on the trail, using an older seasoned horse for a lead makes good use of natural horse behavior. Where the older horse goes the younger horse is likely to follow even through that hazardous crater of molten lava we call a stream. The trick to getting this to work is to keep the youngster close to the lead horse. Before the fearless trail horse plunges into the water, get the nose of the colt right up beside his teacher. Most of the time, as the old campaigner crosses the obstacle, he will take the green colt with him.

The more green horses, the better. Keep them bunched up and pushing on each other, driving the horse in front along. Should a colt quit the herd, send the lead horse back and let them buddy up again before attempt-

23

During the early training of a green colt out on the trail, using an older seasoned horse for a lead makes good use of natural horse behavior.

ing the obstacle

The disposition of the lead horse does make some difference. Horses have a space around their bodies that they protect; this is their personal space. A good pony horse allows other horses into his personal space and communicates a protective nature.

This bearing reminds young horses of the attitude of their mothers. Up close next to her, they felt protected from life's challenges. In this position they followed their dams wherever she led them.

At first it's the pony horse's job to lead. But soon it must become your job. You must develop enough trust and respect from the young horse that he will go anywhere you ask. He must learn to believe that you have stepped into the shoes of a herd leader. Then he will willingly look to you to arrest his fears about spooky things like linen table cloths and molten lava streams.

Up close to their dams, foals feel protected from life's challenges. In this position, they follow wherever the mare goes.

CHAPTER 4

Hang Ups, Obsessions and Fetishes

My horse is terrified of white tail deer . . .
                                        Diana

. . . (my horse) is very shy and skittish of automobile traffic.

                                        Will

(My horse) gets very hyper, upset and nervous on the trail. . . .The real problem hits when we're walking down a slow-traffic road and a medium-sized truck will come along. She'll immediately freeze and then start to run away, prancing and jumping every which way.
                                        Lara

Does it seem that cars, trucks, trains, deer and other assorted "boogymen" have put a curse on your horse? Behind every tree, around every curve, they hide, just waiting to spook the poor unsuspecting creature upon which you sit.

What makes a horse behave like this? Is he a "fraidy-cat?" Does he have a deep rooted problem caused by a bad experience? Is his rider causing the problem or is Mother Nature to blame? While fears and phobias may look the same to the novice student of equine behavior, the causes and cures are vastly different. The first step to fixing the problem begins by plugging into the equine mind.

Understanding this basic mind set of horses gives us insight into why horses behave as they do. How we handle these natural expressions of "horseness" will determine how the horse will react the next time a similar situation arises.

Consider Diana's horse who is afraid of white tail deer. Diana's letter detailed her solution for solving this problem: she turned the mare out in a pasture known to be frequented by deer. This might seem like a plausible solution; unfortunately, it is not likely to work. It is not natural for horses to be scared of deer. It's more probable that SOMETHING caused this horse to begin behaving this way.

To get to the root of the problem, we need the answer to the following question: does the horse spook whenever she sees a deer or only when she is being ridden and sees a deer?

If this horse gets upset at the sight of a deer regardless of where or what she is doing, then we probably have a horse with a deer phobia. But if this horse only gets upset by the sight of a deer while being ridden, we can speculate how this might have begun. Perhaps it went like this:

Diana was riding along the trail one day when a spooked deer jumped out of the brush. (Deer are not terribly fearful of horses and they don't necessarily avoid them when running to escape from a predator.) The quick movement out of the thicket caused her horse to momentarily tense up and lunge sideways. Diane, on the other

In a herd, if one horse senses something out of the ordinary, he will immediately tense up as all his senses hone in on the distraction.

hand, was twice spooked. She jumped from the appearance of the deer and then got upset by her horse's response. Unfortunately, Diane's reaction only served to get her horse more upset.

This is a part of normal horse behavior that it is extremely important for every rider to understand. Horses are very tuned into tension that is created by apprehension. In a herd, if one horse senses something out of the ordinary, he will immediately tense up as all of his senses hone in on the distraction. Instantaneously, a wave of alertness will move through the rest of herd as the members await the sentry's decision. Within just a moment, one of two things will happen. The sentry will either judge the encounter as unworthy of further attention, or he will become increasingly tense as he continues to watch the potentially dangerous intrusion.

All of this happens in less time than it just took you to read about it. When the sentry is no longer interested in the event, his body relaxes and he returns to his previous behavior, grazing, resting or moving about slowly, and the herd follows suit. If the opposite is true and the sentry is convinced of a "clear and present danger," a ripple of energy will explode through the herd as they dart to a safer location, following his lead.

This behavior is part and parcel of the horse. Nothing we do can change his fundamental nature, but understanding how the horse is programmed to react will allow us to manipulate his normal behavior to our advantage. Let's return to Diane's problem and use this information to further investigate her predicament.

When Diane got double spooked by her horse's behavior, she signaled to the mare that the event was a potentially dangerous situation from which they might want to escape. This caused her horse to get even more excited, a reaction which caused Diane to get even more tense. By the time Diane got herself and her horse calmed down, the damage had been done to the horse's attitude towards deer. Each subsequent deer encounter is likely to get worse as Diane's tension feeds her horse's reaction.

Breaking the cycle is not going to be easy. While it is possible that Diane might have taught her horse to be afraid of deer, it is more probable that she has taught the mare that she, Diane, is afraid of deer. Diane has become the sentry in her horse's view and the mare is reacting to the sentry's fear. To change the response, Diane must react like a horse. When startled by a deer, initial tension is expected. But after a quick assessment of the situation, Diane must relax and ride on, a clear message that deer are not to be feared.

We know that this is a lot easier said than done, but the following story will show how perceptive horses are to a rider's fears. Several years ago, a novice rider's horse seemed to get increasingly upset about traffic passing by as he was ridden along the road. After watching to see exactly what was going on, it was obvious that the nervous one in this pair was the rider. This attitude was expressed by her alertness to possible encounters with motorized vehicles. She was constantly on guard, eyes peeled and ears tuned — a pose not unlike that of the attentive herd sentry. When she sensed an approaching vehicle, the rider would tighten up the reins and move the horse as far away from the road as possible. The horse, spooked by the rider's apprehension, became tense and "high" — an act which caused the rider to become more and more sure that her apprehension was justified.

As might be expected, it became harder and harder for this team to join any rides with roadside sorties. Then an interesting thing happened. The horse arrived for a trail ride with a new passenger, an equally novice rider but one without any knowledge of the horse's so-called fear of cars. Not once during that ride did the horse get upset by passing cars or trucks. Of course, neither did his new rider!

This is just one of many examples that we could have told to illustrate the point that riders' fears are reflected in their horses' behavior. Over and over we see horses that refuse to cross creeks, bridges, ditches and countless other obstacles for one rider, only to fearlessly navigate the barrier for another. This can be extremely frustrating for all horsemen, and one to which one of us (Lynda) can personally testify:

My own test by fire occurred in my early twenties as I was breaking my first horse. My premier challenge was provided by a very intelligent Arabian mare who, for nearly thirteen years, had managed to convince humans that she was unbreakable. At the ripe old age of fifteen, she had quite

31

a bag of tricks at her disposal. While she was basically not nice to be around in any circumstance, she saved her "best trick" for those who lacked good sense and tried to get on her back: she flipped over.

To say that I was apprehensive about cutting my teeth on this mare would be an understatement. Yet, the die had been cast and my lot was drawn. Many times during my twelve week involvement with this mare, I found myself pulled into situations that were choreographed by my apprehensions. Initially, like many people, I refused to believe that I created the problems and placed the blame on the horse. Then came the day that reality hit me square in the face.

On this particular day I was trying to ride the mare in a small rectangular pen. The arena was surrounded on all four sides and three of the corners by various buildings. The remaining corner was open and became the battleground for the session.

Starting to work at a walk, I thought the mare seemed to shy slightly in this open corner. My fears were realized as our speed increased. As we broke into a trot, the mare began to tense up and duck out of the corner.

Accordingly, my apprehension grew as I wondered what would be my torment for the day. To date, the mare had sent me to the hospital with a telescoped spine after pitching me 15 feet in the air, not to even mention all the other numerous scrapes and bruises. So, as we approached the corner, I got ready for whatever she was going to pull.

After a few rounds at the trot, the mare navigated the corner perfectly. Then we picked up the canter. The first round the mare jumped five feet sideways out of the corner. Upset but determined, I tried to work her in small circles in the problem area of the ring. Each time she reached the corner, she jumped further and further sideways. Within a few minutes, my nerves were fried and my fragile confidence gone. Scared to death, I stopped the mare and got off. Being human, I immediately screamed at my mentor (who happens to be the coauthor of this book) about what he could do with this mare and how I hoped I never saw her again.

Before I could get out of sight, Jim hopped off the fence, swung up on the mare, kicked her off into a lope and proceeded for THE CORNER. To my utter amazement, the mare cantered around the pen and through the corner perfectly. Around and around the pen they cantered. The mare never threatened, or even hinted that she might jump, shy or otherwise spook.

In humiliation, I watched, knowing that the mare had read my fear and used it to win another victory. As the realization sunk in, my fear turned to anger — not anger at the mare, but anger at myself. I had let my fear of the unknown rule my behavior. I was afraid of what the mare might do — not what she was actually doing at the moment. This tension alone created the problem.

I called for the mare. Still respectful of her devious nature, but filled with anger at myself, I remounted the equine Beelzabub and kicked her into a lope. As we approached the corner, I dared her to try anything. She cantered just like an old broke horse around the curve. I remember her resulting "new" attitude to this day, and the lesson I'll never forget.

Fortunately, it is not necessary to train on the fields of Armageddon to learn that the first place to look for the root of a horse's problem is within yourself. Horses provide a mirror through which you see a reflection of your own fears and insecurities. The hardest step is to stop and look. No one wants to admit that he or she is scared. It is much easier to blame the horse. However, until we are willing to deal with our own insecurities, it is unrealistic to expect our horses to be more confident than we are.

Horses do take on the personalities of their trainers. A nervous rider makes for a skittish horse. A confident rider contributes to a calm horse. Don't let the old saying that "there are none so blind as those who will not see" apply to you.

Begin the search for the root of your horse's problem by looking within yourself. Your efforts will be rewarded as you progress towards the ultimate goal of all equestrians, "to ride as one with a horse."

CHAPTER 5

Horse Phobias

Charlie was a strange horse for a ranch gelding. He was part Saddlebred and part Tennessee Walking Horse. His gaits were wonderful, but his mind wasn't wound tight. Bridges were his special nightmare. The wooden boards giving under his weight. The clanging of his shoes along the metal braces. When it got too much, Charlie'd just pass right out!

And don't make the mistake of shooting a gun off of him. No sooner would the gunshot be heard than poor Charlie would collapse right out from under you, completely dead to the world — adding terror to confusion making you think that your bullet had ricocheted and struck him.

Horses, like people, come in all sizes, shapes and dispositions. Generalities describe groups, not individuals. Yet understanding all the possibilities that exist within the horse population makes it easier to explain the behavior of one individual, say, your horse. In the last chapter, we examined how horses mirror your fears and insecurities. Now we are going to discuss horses that have phobias of their own, an affliction that demands a very different approach.

The Webster's definition of phobia, "a persistent, abnormal or illogical fear of a specific thing or situation," doesn't even come close to expressing the irrational behavior that a horse can exhibit when a phobic fear pulls his trigger. Horses in this state can show behavior that is crazy, suicidal, frenzied, and completely out of control. They might try to run straight through solid walls in an attempt to get away from the object of their fear or, in a moment of terrifying confusion, run right at the very thing that scares them the most.

As trainers and students of horse behavior, we have been introduced to more than our fair share of phobic horses. Most of the time it is possible to lay the blame for the problem on an abnormal experience in the horse's past. For example, there was the mare that went ballistic whenever she was mounted. She had been forced to let big circus cats jump onto her back. Or the horse that hit stall walls hard enough to knock himself out when being cinched up after being brutally traumatized during his first saddling. But the horse that had been hit by a car as a yearling created a most dangerous situation.

We bought this horse through a sale where he was advertised as a green broke two-year-old. Since the words "green broke" mean anything from "a horse has been saddled once" to "a horse who has been ridden many times but does not have a lot of upper level schooling," we assumed that the horse was not broke and started his training at the beginning. He was well schooled in all the basics. So after several days of riding in pens and rings, we felt it was time to test his trail sense.

A group of about ten horses at various stages of training was put together and we headed off for our favorite trail, down the road to the power lines and open spaces.

Initially, the young gelding rode as expected, following some of the older horses around and through various obstacles until we reached the road. As the group began to ride down the side of the road, the young horse become increasingly excited. Riders on seasoned, calmer horses formed a line along the edge of the road, placing themselves between the gelding and the road. The gelding's fretfulness subsided but, unfortunately, a curve in the road made it necessary for the horses to break rank and ride single file. The youngster was placed in the middle of the pack where we hoped that the older horses would continue to influence his behavior.

Then, about halfway through the curve, we found out exactly what was causing the young horse to behave in such a manner. As we heard the sound of a big truck downshifting to negotiate the curve, the colt began to knock into horses as he tried to get away from his fear. The trucker, seeing the commotion, laid on his air horn. The youngster leaped into the air as he tried to jump directly into the path of what was causing his terror.

With tenths of seconds seeming like hours, we watched helplessly in horror. This day made true believers of all of us in the super physical strength one receives from an adrenaline surge. Mid-air in the jump, Jim hit the colt with his spur hard enough to change his direction in mid-flight. Instead of jumping into the path of the oncoming truck, the young colt flew over a metal guard rail; Jim and the horse fell about five feet into a honeysuckle and briar patch. We later learned about his accident as a yearling, the cause of his fear.

This is the kind of unthinking, out of control behavior that a horse with an "abnormal or illogical" phobia can exhibit. Retraining these horses, if they are worth the risk to human life, is something few relish. It is dangerous and hazardous.

Being tangled up with vines, thorns and an angry Irishman made this horse think twice about losing his wits. His behavior steadily improved, but it would have been foolhardy for any rider ever to trust him in traffic.

Fortunately, few horses are born with phobias. On the other hand, many horses have some innate fears that must be handled properly so that the fear will disappear rather than magnify itself. Aversion to loud noises, quick movements, restraint, and pressure around the girth are some of the environmental triggers which cause reactions in a large portion of the horse population. Individual responses range from a moment of stress to completely wild, destructive behavior. Most of the time, the choice of which reaction occurs is yours.

Over the evolution of horse training, two schools of thought have developed to "train" horses to overcome their fears. Each technique is well known in psychological circles: one is called *flooding*, the other *desensitization*. To illustrate the difference between the two techniques, let's consider how each approach would deal with the same problem: cinching up a young colt for the first time. Those that believe exclusively in flooding would restrain the horse so that the cinch can be done up. This might involve the use of hobbles, cross chains, or just pulling the cinch on a seemingly very docile colt. The thing these saddling routines have in common is that they present the new experience of being cinched up all at once. The horse is forced to deal with his fear all at once. It's the old "sink or swim" philosophy applied to horse training.

Fortunately, many horses are not very sensitive to girth pressure. However, for the ones that are, a crucial moment in their life has just occurred. Phobic fear overpowers their bodies, and they can expend every ounce of energy in their thousand pound bodies trying to escape from the terror.

The outcome of this event will make a lasting impression on their lives. If the horse exhausts his energy and still finds himself girthed up, he has the opportunity to learn that the cinch will not hurt him. On the other hand, if he is successful in removing the root of his panic, his phobia becomes more confirmed and his behavior more irrational. There is the possibility that the horse could injure himself, even fatally, by breaking a leg, or by receiving a lethal blow to the head after rearing up and falling over backwards.

Cinching up for the first time would be handled in a completely different manner by those trainers who practice desensitization. Desensitization requires that new and potentially fearful situations be introduced to the horse in small increments. This allows the horse to deal with a potentially frightening stimulus in small doses before he has to handle the entire event.

A desensitization program for heartgirth pressure might involve the following steps:

Begin with a lead rope wrapped around the heartgirth and slowly drawn tight. If the horse begins to become anxious or to show other signs of discomfort, the pressure is reduced to a level acceptable to the horse. Slowly, the idea of increasing is presented, building on the horse's acceptance of the last step.

Next, a surcingle is used to allow the horse to move while experiencing this kind of pressure. In the beginning the surcingle is loosely attached and tightened slightly as the horse accepts each stage of pressure. Only after the horse is completely comfortable with the tightened surcingle would the saddle be introduced.

In complete opposition to the "sink or swim" theory, desensitization tries to avoid stress and fear. It seeks to introduce in increments the sensations that might trigger a horse into phobic behavior. Psychological research in this area has confirmed what many horsemen have known intuitively for a long time: desensitization is a positive approach to training that minimizes the negative side effects produced when an animal is forced to deal with a fearful situation.

Let's look at the basic steps to creating a desensitization program.

1. Identify exactly what is causing the fear. Most of the time, the situation creating stress for the horse is related to one of those innate triggers, such as restriction of freedom, quick movements, loud noises, fear of the unknown, etc.

2. If possible, break the potentially fearful event down into component parts and desensitize each component separately. This means looking at the experience from the horse's point of view; consider all the new sensations that this event will possibly present to the horse. Then, begin with the element you think will cause the least stress. Once this sensation no longer causes anxiety, move on to the next potentially stressful component. Only after the horse has accepted all of the parts is it the time to present the total event.

3. Present each potentially fearful sensation first at a level that minimizes the negative responses from the horse. When the horse is comfortable with the new stimulus, the intensity can be increased gradually, moving to the new level only after the horse shows he can handle each increment.

4. Complete each step on both sides of the horse's body. Don't think that because he accepts the pressure on the left side he will accept it on the right as well. Each side of the horse's body is different. He may be comfortable with the object on one side and still be afraid of the experience on the other. This possibility highlights the

fact that it may be harder to desensitize one side than the other, but that only means that it may take longer to desensitize one side. Take the needed time and don't move on until the horse is completely desensitized on both sides. The end results will be well worth your effort.

To help put this program into practice, let's tackle a common training problem, that of clipping a horse for the first time.

1. **Identify the problem.**

It is not precise enough to say that a horse is apprehensive about clippers. Most horses show curiosity towards the silent, cold, steel clippers in your hands. It is only after electricity activates the mechanical device that most horses become wary. Therefore, the problem is really *running* clippers.

2. **Break the event into component parts.**

Two things occur when the clippers are turned on: a sound is generated and a vibration is created. A horse can accept these attributes of clippers, but touching his body with the machine brings new sensations to his mind. So we have basic sound and vibration, along with sound and vibration touching his skin.

3. **Present the fearful sensation at a minimal level.**

Begin by letting the horse examine the deactivated clippers. Hold them where he can see them and then bring them closer so that he can smell them or lip them. Once his curiosity is satisfied, rub the clippers over his body. This will get him used to the feel of the machine, minus the sound and vibration, against his body. It shouldn't take very long before he becomes nonchalant about what you are doing.

Now it's time to turn them on. It is difficult to present the sound or vibration in varying increments unless you have a variety of sizes of clippers. One way to approach the problem is to hold the noisy tool at an acceptable distance from his body, a distance where the noise and vibration doesn't cause him any distress.

Once he is no longer startled by the noise, work with the horse until you can bring the clippers in close for his examination. Only after he has had the opportunity to examine the device should the vibrating piece of equipment be placed next to his body.

There are several good places to begin. Clipping can occur around the muzzle as the horse examines the equipment with his lip, or around the barrel or heartgirth. You don't actually have to let the clippers shave the hair, just to allow him to get used to the feel of the clipper before you go to the sensitive areas such as the legs and ears.

4. **Don't forget to work through each step on both sides of his body.**

Using this approach it may take three or four days to work through the full program on a horse who is afraid of buzzing sounds and vibrations (cotton in the ears is a good idea for all horses being clipped). But your patience will be rewarded. The next time you clip your horse, he will be less afraid of what is going to happen. In fact, most horses can become so desensitized to the sights and sounds of the clippers that they can be clipped without any form of restraint at all.

It depends on you. Remember, initially, all it takes is a little time and patience to develop and implement a desensitization program to work around most horses' innate fears. It is a whole lot easier to teach a horse he has nothing to fear than it is to convince him that he really isn't afraid of whatever it is he perceives as threatening.

At the end of every desensitization program comes the moment of truth: the time comes to present the dreaded object, full-blown, in all its glory. Now, we would be negligent if we let you think that each and every desensitized horse willingly submits to the object. It just doesn't happen that way in the real world. Some horses do calmly accept the new experience and the rest have varying levels of apprehension. For these, we hope the desensitization process has prepared them to handle the full-blown experience without becoming a threat to themselves or you. The hope is that their reactions will be less violent so they can learn from the experience, instead of being consumed by their desire to escape.

Experience is the best teacher of when to move from desensitization to flooding, but there are some guidelines that might help you. As long as the horse is making progress in accepting the new stimulus, desensitization is working. However, watch out for horses reaching a plateau. When their progress levels out, you will see their attitude change. They will no longer be trying to learn, but instead will show signs of rejection. Fear will return to their eye as they become increasing sure that they want no part of the object. When this happens, it is time to present the object. Continuing to desensitize will only serve to make the horse more afraid and more convinced he should try to get away.

Part of the procedure of making a well-schooled horse is to eliminate this attitude. A horse must learn that he has to override his natural instincts of "fight or flight." He must submit to the pressures placed upon him by his human partner.

For those horses who can't be totally desensitized, restraint may be necessary to bring them to this acceptance. Restraints take many forms but the purpose is to convince the horse that he must handle the pressure. In the case of the horse being clipped for the first time,

POSSIBLE DESENSITIZATION PROGRAMS

Identify the Problem	Break into Components	Steps to Desensitization
Injections	1. Standing in the correct position.	1. Pat neck with hand until horse ignores movement.
	2. Arm movements associated with needle insertion.	2. Pinch skin at site until horse ignores.
	3. Bee sting sensation	3. Cover eye so horse can't see arm movements or needle.
Gun being shot off by rider	1. Sound	1. Put cotton in his ears.
		2. Begin on the ground with a pump B-B gun at a distance that doesn't bother the horse.
		3. Gradually move towards horse, increasing sound of shot by pump-ing up the gun.
		4. As he accepts each level of sound, move to larger calibers.
		5. Repeat the process while mounted.

44

restraint might take the form of a stock; for the cinchy horse, it may be a longe line.

Ultimately, the goal of all training techniques is to develop respect and trust from the horse. Horses respect power. Being able to place limits on a horse's reactions during times of stress demonstrates that you have this power. Judicious use of this power convinces the horse that you are one to be trusted. These approaches to desensitizing specific problems are just suggestions. It is necessary to develop an individual program for your horse that deals with his own unique fear and apprehension. As always, the bottom line is "Listen to your horse." He will show you exactly where his insecurities lie. Then it is your job to show him that there is nothing to fear.

CHAPTER 6

A Battle For Dominance:
The Barn Sour Horse

My four-month-old colt just started throwing tantrums when I lead him away from the barn. When he thinks we've gone far enough, he'll turn and bite at me, then try to run away. When I try to stop him, he'll jump up. After he's calm, I'll try leading again, but he insists we've gone far enough.

He ties up and ponies real good, and he'll even lead okay for a short distance like into his stall or out of the barn. But when I try to lead him any farther, like to another paddock, he blows up. I get after him when he's tied up or in his stall for nipping and he knows its wrong. I can't understand his behavior. He's almost to my shoulders now, so he's getting too big to play these games.

Tina

"After ten years of studying equitation, I decided I was ready to own my first horse. After much searching, I found Mandy, a green broke-two-year old with a wonderful disposition. Mandy and I got along great until I decided she was ready to leave the rings and paddocks around the barn and head out for her first trail ride. She threw a fit: balking, rearing and running backwards.

For the last ten months I have tried to deal with the problem by letting her follow other horses away from the

barn, or leading her out of sight of the barn before I get on.
Success has been limited. When Mandy decides she has
enough, she begins her fit-throwing routine. If I can't ride
Mandy on the trail, how will I ever make it to the show ring?
Barbara

Both these horses are exhibiting the fundamentals of barn sour behavior. Even at the tender age of four months, Tina's weanling is giving its owner the same message as the older riding horse that bucks, jumps, balks or otherwise refuses to leave the barn area. To us humans, these horses seem stubborn, obstinate, unruly and uncooperative. They are, but let's delve deeper and explore some of the reasons why these behaviors occurs in the first place.

For horses who live in or around a barn, the place takes on a special meaning. Restricted by fences, the barn becomes the very center of their horse world: a specific location that serves as a focal point for the herd. A horse refusing to leave the barn is actually objecting to leaving the herd. His behavior is an expression of his refusal to accept you as the dominant member of your herd of two. He fights to return to his equine herd and rejects your dominance by refusing to go off with you.

Tina's weanling is definitely testing his position in the dominance hierarchy with humans and Tina is losing. If Tina could convince the young horse that she is as dominant as the foal's mother, or even the pony horse the foal is willing to go off with, he would go anywhere she wanted. Since she hasn't, the colt has devised a series of behaviors to thwart and frustrate her attempts to lead him (or, in his mind, to dominate him). Although the behaviors of the youngster may seem different from those chosen by the older riding horse, the thought pattern is the same: "what can I come up with that my rider can't handle so

48

This youngster is balking as he is led from the barn, reluctant to leave his "herd" and not accepting the handler as the dominant member in the herd of two.

that I can get my way (dominate) and return to the barn (herd)?"

The solution for both situations is the same. You must prove to the horse that you can and will handle whatever he throws at you and win the battle. That will give you the advantage in proving to the horse *you* are the dominant member of your herd of two.

Begin by breaking your horse's tantrum into specific behaviors. You can then devise a response to each that enables you to eliminate that behavior. After all, there are only a limited number of things that a horse can do to refuse to leave the barn.

If you can handle each of his little tricks, all will be lost from his perspective and your problem will be solved. Let's use Tina's colt as an example.

Trick # 1: "turns and bites at me."

Biting is *never* an acceptable behavior. Tina knows

49

that because she gets after him when *he is tied up or in his stall*. What Tina doesn't know but the colt does, is that she doesn't reprimand him for biting when out in the open. He knows that it is wrong and that he should be punished for it — he runs backwards after the attempt — but Tina doesn't have a foolproof response to fend off his trick whenever it happens.

Scolding a potentially unruly colt out in the open can be somewhat tricky. One sure way to handle this problem is to prevent it from happening. This could be accomplished by using a leather muzzle which attaches to the halter and covers the mouth. The colt can still try and bite but all attempts will be unsuccessful.

Note: This technique will not correct the problem; it just eliminates the possibility.

A true solution might be found in a number of ways. Gelding the young stallion will remove some of his desire to bite. Stallions tend to have an oral fixations. They like to bite; it's part of their play behavior which eventually allows them to become herd masters. Castration will fix some of the problem but, ultimately, the solution rests with the owner being able *always* to maintain the discipline that she will not allow the horse *ever* to bite at her.

This foal's dam would not tolerate him biting on her. Neither should Tina! Smacking at him and missing is not the answer. Remember, biting is a colt game. He thinks you are just playing the game. Fussing and half-heartily picking on him for biting is worthless. The law must be written: THOU SHALT NOT BITE OR YOU SHALL PAY THE PRICE. A bite for a bite. Perhaps a lead with a chain under his chin could convince him he doesn't want to bite. It is going to take aggressive responses which the colt will accept as punishment to eliminate this behavior. He must become more scared of what will happen if he bites you than the fun he is having biting and watching your flailing response.

Trick # 2: "(after trying) to slap him, he jumps up."

This probably means that he rears up — another favorite colt move designed to intimidate his playmates. Snatching on a chain run under the chin is also likely to cause this colt to rear. This might be eliminated by placing the chain over the top of the nose, but this colt is probably going to rear anyway. It's part of the game he is now playing so that he doesn't have to leave the barn.

Rearing tends to scare folks and this colt may be getting a big kick out of his owner's frustration and fear from his trick. But there is an equalizer: rearing puts a horse at a disadvantage. Standing up on two hind legs, a horse is not able to move quickly in any direction while humans are quite agile on their two legs. By quickly moving down the side of a rearing horse, it is possible to smack his belly with the end of lead rope or a crop. You will be amazed how quickly rearing can be eliminated if a horse gets a wallop on his belly each time he goes up in the air.

Trick # 3: "After he's calm, I try leading him again."

Getting your owner to let you calm down and regroup can become the prime object of a series of negative behaviors. Yes, horses that are scared don't always think as clearly as calm ones but if the colt isn't scared, he is just playing a game to get his owner to back off. If this colt can't bite and rearing is no longer an option, perhaps leading like a little gentlemen will become his next best option. But our best guess is that before he gives up completely, he is going to try running backwards.

Running backwards is another maneuver designed to

throw a wrench in the best of plans. However, horses can't run backwards very fast or for very far. The thing you don't want to do is to run straight at them as they run backwards. This makes them back up faster and further.

To beat this trick, it is necessary to get out to the side and swing the horse off balance so that you control the direction of his backward moment. With a little practice, it is easy to have the colt moving backwards in the direction that you want him to go. If he won't move forward away from the barn, backing away is a good second choice.

It is a lot harder to move backwards than forwards, a fact that most horses will quickly acknowledge. When the point has been made, try to lead him in a normal fashion. It may take several tries, but if you persevere you can't lose.

The tricks of Tina's weanling are not very much different from the ones that Barbara's barn sour filly is throwing at her: rearing, bucking, and running backwards. And the responses that will solve Barbara's problems are very similar to the ones already suggested.

Running backwards is probably the easiest to handle. By using the reins, bring the head around and the body will rotate. In the blink of an eye, the barn sour horse will be backing away from the barn.

Rearing and bucking are more difficult to handle, especially if you are a novice. There are many reasons why horses choose one of these behaviors but, for now, let's assume that the horse is doing his trick to refuse your dominance order to leave the barn. What to do depends upon the truthful answers to the following two questions:

1. **Is the horse trying to hurt you?**

If you answered yes, please get someone to help you.

A horse that is definitely trying to hurt you should be sold or sent to a professional trainer, one that can fix the problem both for himself and *you*.

2. Are you scared when the horse behaves like this?

A horse knows when you are scared. This knowledge becomes valuable information as it indicates to him which trick to use to intimidate you. You can count on his using this maneuver whenever he wants to challenge your dominance. It becomes a tactic to manipulate YOU into giving him HIS way. Unless you can overcome your fear, you will find it extremely difficult to fix the problem. Fear causes you to freeze. Your reaction time will be down. Your ability to think clearly will be muddled. All are repercussions that give the horse the upper hand.

If you truthfully answered no to the above questions, let's devise some counter-actions which remove the opportunity for rearing or bucking to occur. Spinning or moving in a tight circle is a favorite. Like running backwards, it takes more energy to move in a small circle than straight ahead. A sharp quick jerk to the head will convert the start of a rear or buck into a maneuver that is a lot easier to ride.

Don't be in too big a hurry to let the horse return to a normal forward moving mode. A tight circle can be transformed into a bigger and bigger circle as the horse becomes more and more willing to want to do as the rider desires. If an argument develops, the circle can quickly be reduced.

Horses are not dumb animals. In fact, in many cases they seem to be smarter than a lot of the folks that are trying to train them. You must take the time to work on the troubling behaviors, have an arsenal of responses ready, and be willing to implement them. The worst

53

thing you can do is quit. The horse wins and he *knows* it. The next time the battle will be bigger because he *knows* he can win again.

Some other keys to dealing with these problems are:

Don't tackle the problem unless you have the time. Be willing to take five or six hours to convince the horse that you can make him walk to a paddock. If it only takes 30 minutes, great, but be ready to devote the time to win the battle.

Don't get frustrated! You begin to lose when you show this expression to the horse. Stop and think the trick through and devise an approach which will work before he tries it again.

Be ready for the horse to change his act. Think ahead and have solutions ready before he even tries a new trick. The confidence you display will be evident to him.

And last but not least, **don't get mad — get even!** Win fairly by beating the horse at his own game and the spoils to the victor will be respect and submission from a horse that will be willing to go anywhere you ask.

CHAPTER 7

The Bucking Horse

A rippled explosion of energy, a mind oblivious to time and space, each jump accompanied by a hoarse squall — an objection from the soul. This horse is bucking for survival.

Head attached to a weaving, snaky neck, eyes dancing with play, ears twisting and turning, pulsing muscle tone, jumping, prancing, popping up in the hind end. This is playful bucking.

Head dropped down to knee level, pinned ears, clinched teeth, tense muscles, a cold, unyielding glare. This is 'refusal' bucking.

What makes a good cowboy movie? Good horses ridden by fair actors and one fine bucking scene. Remember *The Cowboys* with John Wayne where the uppity young cowhand rode the bronc that bucked off the rest of the boys? Or when Lee Marvin busted up the town as he rode The Gray in *Monte Walsh*. And who can forget the sequence in the television miniseries *Lonesome Dove* as Call conquered Hell Bitch. Yes, there is something incredibly exciting about watching a thousand pound animal leap, twist and pound the ground in an all-out effort to remove from his back the human animal that seeks to dominate his soul.

Yet the romance of the old West quickly disappears when it is *you* astride one of these mighty awesome creatures! It seems that most of us do not get a thrill out of doing the bronc-stomping ourselves, but would rather live vicariously through our Sunday matinee idols. The key word here is *live*. Bronc stomping is not for the inexperienced, the fragile or most folks over forty. In fact, unless you want to be a rodeo bronc rider, you should never have to ride a bucking horse.

"Thou shalt not buck with a rider on your back" is one of the Horse Ten Commandments. We consider an older riding horse that bucks to be poorly trained, a young horse that bucks with a rider on his back to have been handled incorrectly. The thought of bucking a rider off should never occur to a horse who is not a part of rodeo's bronc string.

Most of the time it doesn't, but if your horse bucks, you need to know the reason behind it. There are triggers which cause horses to react by bucking, and then there are horses who buck with the intent to do bodily harm. It is imperative to know which category your horse falls into.

The physical maneuver of bucking is as much of a part of how horses move as walking, trotting and cantering. Foals, only hours old, on wobbly legs, test out their ability to buck and jump. Soon they will be racing across the pasture, bucking and kicking to let the world know how great it is to be a horse— alive, athletic, healthy and strong. Bucking can be an expression of the joy of life, or an instinctive survival reaction. Designed by Nature to propel predators off their backs, young horses innately buck from fear.

These two reasons explain much of the horse's bucking behavior up to the time that Man enters the picture.

Phobic fear of girth pressure has caused this young horse to buck.

Then a third reason for bucking often appears. Roped up, tied down, cinched with saddles, girths, bits, tiedowns and other pieces of equipment used for restraint, bucking can quickly become an expression of anger over Man's insensitivity to horses. Once an angry horse bucks off his rider and finds relief from his frustration, he is more likely to use this gift of Nature again to defend against this predator, Man — whenever pushed toward a state of anxiety.

It is absolutely, positively necessary to know which reason explains why a horse is bucking. One solution will not fit every circumstance. Each problem is unique and must be handled individually as well as correctly. As we continue discussing the bucking horse do not lose sight of the fact that horses are individuals. Your horse may be more or less timid than another horse. He may be a slow learner or smarter than some people you know. He may view the world through the eyes of a clown or approach his existence with the seriousness of a Supreme Court

Justice. One solution will not fit every circumstance and a specific solution for a particular problem may not be right for every horse. With that in mind, let's explore the dilemmas created by bucking horses, starting with the one that is easiest to fix.

We all know horses express their natural highs by kicking up their heels. A young horse kept in the stall, well-fed, and bursting with energy is a prime candidate for the title of a "Feel-Good Bucker." These horses aren't directing their energy against you. They aren't trying to buck you off. They expect you to ride their crowhops and back-popping. Should you come off, they seem shocked or bewildered: they don't know how you got on the ground. This exuberance of youth usually disappears by the time a horse is into secondary schooling. If it is a problem, the solution is simple: either turn the horse out and let him burn some energy on his own or longe him before you get on. While both solutions will get the desired results, longing is our personal preference because it allows you to be part of the moment. Sharing life's highs as well as working through the lows is the cement that builds relationships. It is the same with horses as with humans.

Horses that buck from fear are a bigger problem because the solution is unlocked only by knowing *exactly* what the horse is afraid of and desensitizing him to it. Horses, not unlike people, fear what they do not understand. New situations where they do not know what is going to happen or how they should act are just as scary to young horses as they are to children. By taking a little time and gradually introducing a horse to the new experiences associated with breaking, fear-bucking is usually eliminated. In fact, ninety percent of all horses can be broken without ever bucking if they are taught to understand what is being asked instead of just being forced to submit to it.

It would be nice to think that the days are gone when scared-to-death young horses were "bucked out," but we know it is not so. Our barn has a steady stream of horses who arrive with stories like,

"He was so gentle that we tied him up in cross chains and saddled him up. We never thought that he would come unglued. He tore the chains out of the wall and bucked through two fences until the saddle came off".

"I just put the saddle on him in the stall and he threw such a fit that he knocked himself out by hitting the walls."

"The first trainer I took him to tied up a hind foot and got on. When he bucked him off, he wouldn't stand up when they tied up his foot again. So they beat him."

It's too bad that the ancient Greeks didn't have a God to protect horses from people. These horses were scared to death. Saddles, girths and other man-made tack became viewed as items of torture to be avoided at all cost. All of this could have been avoided if only people had taken the time to deal with the horse's intrinsic fears.

To the scared horse, being ridden is not a far cry from having some horse-eating animal clawing into his back. To the attentive equine pupil, the first mounting is an exercise in accepting the weight of a kind, compassionate trainer. One step at a time, the horse learns to accept the new task. First the arms over his back, then a human body lying over his back, and finally a rider astride. If an error in judgment is made and the horse jumps from fear, the compassionate trainer backs off. The fear is removed and the teaching process can begin again. Over the course of a few days, any apprehensions that the horse may have to being ridden have vanished and we have a willing mount who hasn't been traumatized.

Another point that is usually not properly appreciated is that being saddled is very different to a horse than just carrying a rider bareback. Horses must be taught to accept restriction in the heartgirth area because many will buck when the girth grabs them as they move off if they haven't been prepared for this step. In most instances, this bucking response can be eliminated by introducing girth pressure in stages: for example, by taking a rope and holding it snugly around the belly, or by doing a surcingle up a notch at a time. A little patience and understanding goes a long way in easing a green colt through this potentially explosive training session.

On the other hand, we have seen a few horses that have a severe phobia about girth pressure. These horses almost seem to go crazy when the saddle is tightened. When their eyes roll back in their heads and the bellowing begins, it is time to watch out for yourself because these horses have totally lost control. Some primordial genetic program has kicked in and, until deprogrammed, they are a danger to themselves and others who do not understand them.

Then there is the cold-backed bucker: the horse that wants to buck every time a boot is placed in the stirrup and a rider swings onto his back. By definition, these horses' desire to buck is short-lived. Quickly, they turn into willing mounts but the first few minutes can be a nightmare.

Why do they do it? Perhaps these horses carry some psychological baggage from their breaking experiences; maybe they failed to learn there was nothing to fear from being saddled or ridden. Deep in their minds, there is still a part that wants to escape. Each time they are saddled, the hammer is drawn back and the bucking trigger is set to go off.

A common solution for dealing with this problem is to saddle the horse and longe him before mounting. While many riders use this technique to let the horse work through his bucking before they mount, this is also when and where you start to eliminate the problem.

Longe the horse through all his gaits in both directions. Don't be timid. We want him to buck. In order to teach him that the behavior is totally unacceptable, he has to first express it. Any expression of bucking can then be discouraged by the longe whip and strenuous exercise.

Unfortunately, some old, cold-backed sons-of-a-gun have gotten away with this negative behavior for long enough to become too smart: they refuse to come "unglued" unless there is a rider on their backs. This makes the problem much tougher to deal with. Still, there are ways to manipulate the environment enough to set the horse off. Here's what we suggest:

Fill two sacks each with five to ten tin cans. Securely seal the top with a hay string. Now tie the other end of the hay strings to the saddle horn, letting a sack hang off each side of the horse.

Step back and begin longing. Walking and slow turns probably won't create any problems. Be ready when you ask the horse to move faster. The bounce of the stride is going to start the cans banging against each other, hopefully triggering the horse's rejection behavior. As soon as it starts, maintain control by continuing to longe while punishing the horse for bucking and jumping. Some horses may get pretty wild, so we recommend that the procedure be done in a round pen or enclosed area where the horse can't escape or injure himself. And be careful: some horses may come totally unglued and run blindly.

If this works, you have created a situation that resem-

bles the horse's saddling experience. The horse is afraid
and is going to try to escape — only this time we are not
going to let him escape from the situation with any excess
negative baggage. You must longe the horse hard until the
bucking stops. Then continue the session doing   all the
normal maneuvers including hard turns and good stops.
By now you should see the horse trying hard to please
you. Reward this attitude both with verbal praise and by
asking for softer, more relaxed movements.

Each subsequent training session should begin with
the sack-longeing procedure until the horse totally accepts
the cans. Depending upon the horse's nature, this may
happen in two sessions or a week. When it happens, however, the cold-back bucking habit should be gone.

All these examples of bucking horses we've shared up
to this point can be fixed by being a better horseman and
understanding how horses think. But the salty old bronc
who waits for an opportune moment to shed his rider is
another story. This horse has made bucking an art form.
He may wait until you are in the precarious position of
swinging your leg over the back of the saddle in an
attempt to get on. Just as you reach the point of being
committed to mount but have not yet got your seat, pop
goes the weasel — and you're trying to ride a bucking
horse from the three point stance of one foot and two
hands.

Assuming you survived the mounting experience,
and have ridden for several hours, your confidence level
will rise again. In fact you might begin to relax and even
slouch a bit in the saddle. The reins hang loose as you
gaze at some far way object, paying little attention to the
seemingly calm mount you sit astride. Suddenly the "hur-
ricane deck" erupts with the strength of a volcanic explosion. And when the stars clear from your head, old Salty

62

is quietly munching grass just out of range of whatever missile you have that you would like to launch on a seek and destroy mission.

These committed equine bucking artists are the hardest to change because bucking has been such a rewarding pastime for them that it is now an integral part of their relationship with man. It is so etched in to their behavior that it is unlikely you will ever totally be able to erase from their memory the gratification they have gotten from this maneuver.

To extinguish the behavior, you must convince the horse that bucking will cause unpleasant consequences for him instead of for you. The time-honored tradition of the old western cowboy is riding the bronc, whipping and spurring, until the devil disappears. This does work and, if you are cowboy enough to take him on and win, it will probably work for you, too.

However, if the horse is a better bucker than you are rider, which is usually the case, you will need to find another way. One possible solution would be to get off every time your horse went into a bucking fit and give him a good thrashing from the ground. After he has been punished, get back on and begin the riding session again. It may seem harsh, but these horses need to be punished for their actions or else they eventually end up in the killer pen, waiting to be made into dog food.

One of the worst buckers ever sent our way was a three-year-old Appaloosa who had already been sent to four or five trainers. Basically a kind and gentle horse, the first trainer had saddled him up the first day and started to climb on, only to learn too late that this horse had the cinch phobia. Scared to death, the berserk bucker crashed into fences, fell down and flipped over before he tore the saddle loose from his back. Three trainers later, no one wanted to ride this horse. His initial instinctive response now had a learned component. He used his honed bucking skills with expertise. We were his last stop before applying for a job with the local rodeo stock contractor.

The first step was to convince the colt that he *wanted* to carry weight on his back. With no human volunteers, two sacks filled with sand tied together with baling twine became the surrogate rider. With the sacks thrown over his back, the horse was asked to work in a 50 foot breaking pen with seven foot high walls. Every time the bags fell off his back, the buggy whip got the horse. It wasn't long before the bronc understood the concept of keeping his "rider" aboard. In fact, he would get down on his knees to catch the bags or stop dead in his tracks if they began to slip. Then it came time to replace the bags with a real live rider. Within the span of a week, the bronc metamorphosed back into a gentle Appaloosa who now refused to let his rider fall off.

Unfortunately, not all bucking horse stories have such happy endings. Most horses that can't be broke for whatever reason eventually end up in a trailer with a load of horses headed for a meat-packing plant. This is where we came across a beautiful gray half-Arab four-year-old filly with a very unusual story. It was said that she was unbreakable. During the last two years no one had ever stayed on her and she could buck and sunfish with the best of them.

On the ground this mare was a dream. She was kind and gentle, so off to the breaking pen she went. She was willing to learn, and eager to train. Longing went well, bellying over her back was easy. She didn't object to having a rider on her back. She walked off calmly until the rider asked her to turn. Suddenly, all the furies of hell came forth and she bucked the rider off so hard that she

Bendix carrying his sacks of sand.

broke the girl's arm.

The little gray bronc was a puzzle. All of the pieces didn't fit together properly, so we watched her move around the ring. An hour and half later, the light bulb came on: the mare never turned right. Was she blind in the right eye? The eye was clear, but a complete check-up proved otherwise. The little mare was almost blind on that side.

With this new information, we took the mare back to the breaking pen. Again she accepted the rider. This time, however, the rider only asked for left-hand turns. No problem; the mare turned left. The key to the lock had been found. Her training continued for several weeks without a hitch — or a right-hand turn. The mare grew confident in her relationship with humans. Then the inevitable day of reckoning came. Would the mare trust her rider to see to the right for her? Asked to turn right, she yielded the shoulder and moved into the turn like she had been doing it all her life. The last time we heard about the little mare, she was carrying a ten-year-old boy over fences in the hunt fields of Maryland and was the most kind and gentle of mounts.

There are no pat answers for training horses. To understand and communicate with another species takes commitment. Most horses want to please their master. Your obligation is to try and understand them. If your horse bucks from fear, teach him not to be afraid. If he bucks because you have spoiled him and let him be the boss, fix yourself first. If you want your horse to like you, he must respect you. Commitment, trust, and caring all start from this common base. You must be the dominate member of the partnership or you will never experience the joy of riding as one with your horse.

CHAPTER 8

A Rearing Refusal

(Moonshine) is very high-spirited and loves to run. If some other rider tries to catch up with me, he will start to rock, jump and twist in the air — and rear
Beth

(My young filly now) has a habit of biting, kicking or rearing when she doesn't get her own way
Tim

My eight-year-old welsh pony has a bad habit — rearing! For a while my neighbor had her calm (not rearing), but she still rears when she doesn't want to do something
Billy

(Jim) During my early school years, I was sure that my teachers were trying to fool me. They kept trying to convince me that the three "R"'s stood for "Reading, wRiting, and aRithmetic. But my mama didn't raise no fool. I knew what important words started with "R": Riding, Roping and Rodeoing. In fact, I spent all my extra time when they weren't drilling on their R's studying about mine.

This was a harder task than you might think. School days forced me to be in the city while my horses were in the country. Being a weekend cowboy wasn't challenging enough, so I set out to figure how I could ride the horses stabled in town that belonged to other folks. At about eleven years of age, the solution came to me: I could ride all the town horses that no one else wanted to. A perfectly simple answer to my dilemma, I thought.

Being fearless, naive and ignorant, I plunged forward with my plan to further my education in the important three "R"s. Being precocious, however, I quickly learned why these horses weren't being ridden. They each had their own set of tricks which they used to "scare" riders into leaving them alone.

One of the first horses that I got to ride belonged to a classmate of mine. His daddy had bought him a registered Quarter Horse, but my friend wouldn't have anything to do with it. Sure, his dad said, it would be fine for me to exercise his horse. Happy as a lark I set out to catch Charley and ride off into the sunset.

Charley was a fine looking gelding, easy to catch and rode like a dream — that is, until he decided he'd had enough. Suddenly, Charley refused to go. Pounding on his sides produced an unexpected response. The horse reared straight up into the air and leaped forward. Although I was unprepared for the "airs above the ground," they were easy to ride and I stuck with him. The fact that I thought this creative maneuver was fun to ride must have surprised the gelding. It seemed as though Charley figured that either he must not have given the move his best shot, or else it was sheer luck that I stayed on. To test his theory, the little horse proceeded a couple more times to give it his best performance. Finally, Charley decided that his trick wouldn't work on me. He gave up the ghost and went back to doing whatever I asked of him.

From these examples, do you see a pattern emerging?

Within the first few months of age, young males start mock fighting by rearing, pawing and nipping at their playmates.

Rearing is a maneuver commonly used by horses to intimidate their riders. How does it start; why does it work and how do we fix it?

Rearing is a part of the play behavior of young horses. Foals of both sexes run jump and rear as they frolic. Although fillies do rear and paw at each other during moments of spirited play, for colts the move holds more meaning. Days after birth, the male suckling can be found rearing and pawing on his dam's back. Within the first few months, young males start mock fighting by rearing, pawing and nipping at their playmates. The older they get, the rougher the play becomes. This is Nature's way of developing the skills necessary for the stallion to survive in the wild, and even though the wild doesn't exist anymore, the genetic program cannot be overridden.

Play-fighting allows the young horse to learn about himself: where he fits in the herd, how aggressive he is, how much physical strength and coordination he has and the advantages that rearing can give him over weaker

69

adversaries. The better a horse can rear and strike at his opponent, the greater his power. The horse with the most power intimidates all the rest of his buddies.

Foals find this power rewarding, so it is almost to be inevitable that they are going to test out the maneuver on humans sometime during early handling. Nipped in the bud, the young equine will quickly learn that rearing doesn't scare humans any more than it scared his 1000 pound dam when he pawed her in the back.

What we want him to know *is* that the act is going to get him in trouble. His mama didn't tolerate it and neither will we. On the other hand, if the young horse learns that rearing gives him an advantage, this useful information is stored in the back of his mind for future reference. Now the potential exists for the young horse to use this trick anytime he wants to object to what is going on.

Even if the horse made it though his early years without learning that humans could be intimidated by rearing, many novice riders accidentally teach their horses that rearing scares them. Green riders don't always know what their cues mean to the green horse, and a sequence of contradictory cues put the young horse in a vice. This occurs most often during attempts to back up. It seems to work like this: the rider pulls the reins straight back, and fusses if the horse tries to move to either side. To complete the picture, the green rider is probably leaning back in the saddle. The young horse feels trapped. The reins won't let him move forward. He can't go sideways or his sides get banged on. Leaning back in the saddle tells him NOT to move backwards. The only choice left to him is to go up. As he rears, the rider releases the rein pressure.

At first the horse thinks that rearing was the move being requested, but it doesn't take him long to realize that the reaction of his partner is wrong. The rider is not

Some of them even learn to throw themselves over backwards.

pleased. The perceptive horse quickly analyzes the situation and determines the emotional state of his trainer. If his rider is frightened or intimidated, the horse has learned that rearing can be a powerful bad medicine to be used against people just as it is used against other horses.

There are many other ways a horse learns that rearing gives him power over humans, but the thrust of the problem is how to change the horse before the behavior turns into a life-threatening habit. Fortunately, most horses only rear up a little, but a little is all it takes to get the desired result — the rider loses control and doesn't know what to do. For the moment, the horse is in control; he is the dominant member of the riding partnership. He objects, wins and is rewarded just like the play-fighting sessions during his youth. Consistently beat him at his own game and he will give up the behavior.

But beware of the spoiled and confirmed rearer that believes that if a little won't scare you, maybe a lot will.

They get higher and higher with each subsequent rear. Some of them even learn to throw themselves over backwards. These horses are not for novice riders. They can and will hurt you.

We recommend that if you have a horse like this, get professional help immediately. Give the trainer the facts, so he or she can be forewarned. After the trainer has worked with the horse, ask these questions: Is my horse safe to ride? Is he going to try to rearing up with me again? What should I do if he does?

Listen to the answer with an open mind. Don't let your feelings for the horse override your logic. The possibility exists that this type of horse will never be safe for an inexperienced rider. If this is the case, send the horse down the road and buy one that won't hurt you. There is no dishonor in being totally honest about your own abilities, especially with yourself. And, there are thousands of good horses out there that deserve and need a good home.

Fortunately, most horses don't behave like this and removing the rearing habit isn't too hard if you remember a simple concept: *a horse can't do two things at once.* What we want to do is to change rearing into a maneuver which does not have the power to intimidate or hurt us. The easiest swap is to exchange the rear for a spin because both moves start the same way — the horse must rock back on his hindquarters and lift up in front. For right-handed riders, this is easily accomplished by pulling the left rein to the side, causing the horse to bend his head around towards your left leg. At the same time, give the horse a good kick in the right shoulder with your right leg. This will help the horse's front end follow his head to the left — and bring his feet back down on the ground where they belong!

Although it may be beyond the expertise of some

riders to actually teach the spin, a tight circle will work as well. Work the horse in this small circle for several minutes. This action is punishment for the rearing, so you want to make him uncomfortable. You want him to think twice before wanting to rear again. If rearing is his form of refusal, you want the tight circle work to be harder than what he originally refused.

We'd bet money that one time won't fix the problem, so each time he starts to rear be prepared to pull him around and circle him tighter and longer. Stick with this game plan until you have convinced the horse that all attempts to rear will result in him having to do some hard work.

This change in your attitude will convince the horse that rearing no longer intimidates you. You aren't frustrated and aren't at a loss as to what to do. By taking charge of the situation, you gain dominance over your equine partner and move ever closer to achieving the ultimate goal of being one with the horse.

CHAPTER 9

Running Faster Than
You Want To Ride

*I had been riding my gentle two-year-old filly for about
a month when the unexpected happened. Cantering around
the arena, I picked up the inside rein to cut the ring in half.
The filly leaned against the pressure and took off running.
Taken by surprise, I got tense but backed off the pressure and
rode her several rounds before the filly came back to me.*

*This was the easiest filly to break. No buck. No spook. In
fact, I've had her in the woods, squirrel-hunting off of her.
Nothing seemed to bother her. But ever since that day in the
arena, she runs away with me whenever I ask her to do a half
circle at a lope. And today she spooked and ran away on the
trail. I fell off, and broke six ribs and punctured a lung.
Help!!*

Donna

Reschooling the confirmed runaway can be a very
difficult and hazardous retraining problem. The most
dangerous runaway that we've come across was a very talented seventeen hand mare by the name of Pride. Pride
was a first class mover and, at one time, could handily
jump seven feet. Somehow this mare ended up in the
hands of a game but novice rider who rode her in the
hunt field and over fences. Inexperience led to abuse. Her

well-schooled mouth was snatched, bounced, jerked and pulled on. The high-strung filly could not handle the coarseness. She began to crash through fences as she tried to run away from the confusing pain and pressure in her mouth.

When Pride arrived at the farm for reschooling, her mind was ravaged. When first mounted, she began to fret and prance in anticipation of being abused in the mouth. Her immediate response to the slightest pressure on the reins was to turn her chin to the sky and refuse to drop her head. Instantly she got so nervous she lost any willingness or ability to respond. It was like riding a keg of dynamite with a lit fuse. It was only a matter of time until the explosion when Pride rolled her eyes back in her head and took off at a dead run.

Can a horse who has gone this far ever be normal again? No! This mare will always carry the mental wounds created by the trauma. Trust in her rider will always be elusive, and every new rider will have to prove him or herself to her.

Fortunately, most horses who might be classified as runaways don't fall into the same category as this mare. They may only try to run off under certain situations. One of the first steps to fixing the runaway is to understand the behavior. The following examples reveal some common reasons.

The Young, Scared Runaway

Green horses trained and ridden by green riders without knowledgeable instructors have unlimited potential to develop into runaways. The young horse needs security. He needs to know that his pilot is able to handle any situation that may arise. Inexperienced trainers lack the ability to communicate this feeling. The young horse, apprehensive about being out and about in strange places, is on the look out for things that might scare him. Shying and spooking from unrecognizable objects, the green horse desperately needs a rider that can take control of the situation so the horse won't learn he can run away from the things that scare him.

The best solution is prevention: green riders should get older, trained horses. Let experienced horsemen and women ride young horses. This may not be what you want to hear, but it is reality. Early training forms the mind set of a horse for all subsequent training. It is extremely important how horses are ridden for the first year or two. Mistakes leave mental impressions that may limit their usefulness. Unless you have experience dealing with the young equine mind, the methods used in handling the problems can lead to the wrong solutions. For example, the most common strategy used by inexperienced horsemen to correct the problem of the young, scared runaway is to get a stronger bit. Ninety percent of the time, this is the wrong answer!

An experienced horse trainer knows how to bring the young horse through this period of training. It is a traditional practice around many breaking barns to take young colts out on the trail with an older seasoned horse or two. The green horse will follow the "herd." Over the course of several rides, the youngster will gain confidence in himself and learn to ask his rider for instructions as they negotiate obstacles on the trail. The last thing on this colt's mind would be to run away. He wants to be with the herd. As he relaxes, it is easy for an experienced hand to transfer the security that the colt gets from the trail "herd" to himself. The base of trust strengthens.

The Spoiled Horse

Never, never take a horse out and run him from the time you leave the barn until the ride is over. Horses are creatures of habit. Even if the horse is only occasionally treated like this, he is likely to become harder and harder to handle. You have a runaway in the making. Proper horsemanship dictates that a horse should be walked and trotted in circles and figures-of-eight to be warmed up and as stretching exercises. A slow canter continues the process. Only after this progression is finished should the horse be asked for any speed.

And speed is not a tense, nervous effort. A horse needs to learn to run relaxed. Running relaxed provides not only the most efficient movement over the ground, but allows his mind to be receptive towards instruction. Remember, as speed increases, control decreases. A race-horse running 40 miles an hour under the direction of a jockey can weave in and out of horses on the track, but cannot stop, turn around or back up. A frightened speed-crazy runaway has brain-lock. He can't think, he can't turn, he can't stop. He just runs until he feels exhausted.

To avoid getting to this point, speed work for any horse should be followed by a warm-down. Slow cantering, jogging and walking will return the athlete's body and mind to him in a quiet state. The ride will come full circle.

Although this basic procedure should be followed every time, don't do it in the same way or in the same place. Habits are hard to break. A horse can all to quickly learn where to trot and where to RUN. *You* tell the horse when to change gait, not a landmark or location.

Once a horse has become spoiled, how do you change his habits? If you keep him in a stall, turn him out before you ride. Let him burn some of that energy.

Once mounted, ask him to only walk and trot until he is convinced that running is no longer a part of his daily exercise program. It may take a week. It may take a month. But every time the horse moves into a faster gait than was asked for, circle him until he breaks back down to the desired gait.

This is long, tedious schooling process which is not fun on a trail ride. You must be committed to let the others ride off and to work your horse until he is willing to go at *your* speed. It is better to begin the process in a pen or arena. Be ready to pull one rein and get his head around if he tries to run off. Try to circle him the instant that he tries to run of; this is easier than when he's already well underway.

But how you actually get him to give you his head depends a lot on your horse. A steady pull on the reins works for some horses while others only lean on the rein and won't come around. For these horses, which are usually of a stock horse type, snatching or jerking one rein won't allow them to resist and they will follow the pressure.

This snatching or jerking technique drives other horses out of their minds. Many horses with Thoroughbred or running horse breeding can't take this kind of pressure. It only makes them wound up and wanting to run even faster. The sharp jerks seem to chase reality from their minds and they run blindly. It comes back to knowing your horse — the thing that is often most difficult for a novice rider.

The Ex-Racehorse

It is important to remember that horses, unlike roses, are not all the same. The hotter the bloodline, the more instinctive the desire to run. The ex-racehorse usually falls

79

into this category. Techniques to reschool the "Ex" often begin with rebreaking. The horse may know how to carry a human on his back, but turning right and left or stopping and backing may be missing.

When working with an "Ex" highly-energized racing machine, let him burn some off before schooling begins. It is the nature of the hot blooded beast to find it difficult (if not impossible) to think or concentrate as the spirit rises to full power. A little bit of turnout or longeing can work wonders in preventing problems.

Change as many of the conditioned stimuli (the signals that the horse associates with being asked to run) as possible. For example, ride in a western saddle rather than English. Use a curb instead of snaffle bit.

Expect to reschool the ex-racehorse's mouth. He must now learn that the bit is not to lean on in order to go faster. This means that the horse must be backed off the bit. A good training tool that can be used to teach this point is a bitting rig.

The one thing that you must *never* do on any ex-racehorse — or any runaway for that matter — is to haul back on both reins with steady pressure. This kind of pressure in the mouths reminds the horse of racing. It gives him something to lean on to gain momentum. You can not pull a runaway down like this. You must get his head and circle him tighter and tighter until he comes back. Timing is everything. The first runaway stride — *get the head around* — and don't be too gentle. A runaway can hurt himself or you.

The Over-Restrained Horse

There are basically two types of horses that fall into this category. At first glance they appear to be the same, but closer examination of the nuances reveals different

The racehorse is taught to lean into bit pressure.

solutions to the problem.

Type One is the horse that is always ridden with too much constant pressure in his mouth. With the reins choked up and the bit continuously putting pressure on his mouth, this horse is never able to *relax*. It seems like every time he is ridden he gets higher and harder to keep in check. Yet he does have some respect for the bit, so the rein pressure gets greater and greater, and his mouth gets harder and harder. This cycle continues until the horse becomes unmanageable.

The obvious solution begins with the rider giving the horse his head back and allowing him to relax while being ridden. One interesting technique which works on some horses is to let him do what he thinks he wants to do — *run*. However, it is very important that *you* pick the spot for this to happen. The location should have safe footing, but the terrain should cause the horse to work extra hard to run. With these requirements, the locales are limited. Sand dunes, hills, beaches, race tracks and some streams may fit the bill.

Type One is the horse that is always ridden with too much constant pressure in his mouth.

Should you be lucky enough to have a spot for reschooling a runaway in this manner, the procedure is fairly simple. When the horse acts like he wants to run off, let him go. Don't ride tensed up, but let the horse have the impression you want him to run. Try to take back some control by using intermittent bit pressure. When the horse finally decides that he no longer wants to run away, make him go on long enough to convince him that running was not the escape he imagined — it just created more work.

It may take more than just one trip down your race track, but every day should get a little better if this technique is going to work on your horse. Reschooling takes time, but it will be worth it in the end.

And please make careful note of the following: do not use this technique on young, scared horses. You will only make them more frightened. Also, this technique is not a good choice for reschooling the ex-racehorse.

Running far and fast will make them high no matter how hard they work. Finally, never attempt this unless you have a safe place in which to work.

The Type Two over-restrained horse is basically a very light and sensitive individual, more so than Type One. Too much restraint, usually caused by using too strong a bit, makes this horse fractious and high. He tries to escape by running off. Light, sensitive horses need good riders with good hands, not big bits. They are not genetically programmed to be able to handle imbalance and coarseness. Easily schooled by educated horsemen, these horses are very difficult mounts for beginning equestrians. If you think that your horse falls into this category, get help to improve your riding skills and try using a softer bit. Remember, Pride's story began like this. Don't let this situation get out of hand. Consider the fact that you may be over-mounted. The best solution may be to get a horse more suitable to your abilities. This may be a hard decision to make but, in the long run, it will be the best for both you and the horse. A ounce of prevention is better than a pound of cure.

Retraining runaways may require learning better horsemanship. The ideal mount should be relaxed, and ready to perform his rider's command. Riding horses is one of life's great pleasures and many equestrians believe that being aboard a running horse is one of the highest of highs. But unless the horse is a willing and controllable partner during the experience, the team is destined for problems.

So take the time to treat your horse fairly. Warm him up and warm him down. Pay attention to and care about how he feels when he is ridden. Most horses want to do what you ask, so don't abuse that desire. Insist that he take his cues from you, and change gaits only when you ask. The runaway needs to be dominated. He wouldn't run away from the herd, and he shouldn't want to run away from what you want him to do either.

Time, patience and one or two of these reschooling techniques can change most runaways. To make this transformation happen, however, you must not be frightened when the horse tries to run off. If fear paralyzes you, get help rather than struggling on your own. If you have a horse like Pride that is too far gone, get experienced help. But if you understand why your horse wants to run away and the solution to the problem is clear to you, remember this old cowboy saying, "A horse can't run faster than you can ride."

CHAPTER 10

The Fast Track To Ring Sour

. . . taking the bit in his teeth, he crashed through the four foot fence and ran off out of the ring.

Tom

. . . someone has to lead my horse into the ring. She just refuses to get anywhere near the gate

Gayle

Having a horse behave like this can be an embarrassing moment in the life of an equestrian. But the ring sour horse is not to blame. The rider has turned a deaf ear to the admonitions of his horse. Rearing, bucking, running backward, and jumping to the side are some of the ways that horses communicate to their riders that they do not want to do what they are about to be asked to do. Barrel horses and other speed event horses seem to be the most adamant in their dislike about the pending performance. Why do they feel like this? Does speed make them crazy or are they just lazy?

Neither! Pain makes them smart. They do not want to enter into an arena where they are going to be made to hurt themselves by turning barrels, sliding twenty feet, being whipped to run wide open out of the pen only to have to stop short on some hard surface such as gravel.

These are not situations that many horses find fun and rewarding. And the problem is not found only in show horses.

During a trip to Louisiana Downs, we observed a ring sour filly trying to refuse to leave her barn when her race was called. Urged up the road to the saddling paddock, she reared, bucked, and ran backwards at every turn that took her closer to the racetrack where she knew that she was going to have to run or be beaten. Once in the saddling paddock, she threw a fit, jumped out from under the jockey as he was being thrown up and flipped over in the starting gates. She ran dead last.

How do horses get to this point? The answer is almost always bad training! Yet most of these horse owners are genuinely confused about why their horses behave in such a manner. They are often kind and gentle folks who like their horses and wouldn't hurt them for the world. But, obviously, they don't understand what it means to be an equine athlete or how they are torturing their horses.

All athletes, whether human or horse, need to have a warm-up period before they exercise or they can easily tear, rip or strain muscles. Every horse who is tacked up and asked to go right to work risks injury. Walking, jogging, bending and stretching exercises in the form of figure-eights or small circles are a must if a horse is going to be able to perform and not suffer from the effort. This is very different from beating, banging and snatching. The old saying "no pain, no gain" is only partially true. Any horse turning barrels, sliding and turning over his hocks, jumping five feet fences or running 45 miles per hour is going to hurt. How you handle him before and after these efforts will make a difference about how he feels about giving you his best performance. This is what is meant by "keeping his mind right."

Recently we were discussing this very problem with our neighbor Merrill O'Neal, 15 times a barrel racing champion. Having been out on the circuit for the past 25 years, Merrill has seen firsthand most of the ways riders make horses ring sour.

"The biggest mistake I see being made is when a horse that has been running good, suddenly starts refusing to go into the pen. Most owners assume that their horse doesn't want to run anymore and start on whipping him. Experience has taught me that ninety percent of the time when an honest horse starts refusing to run, he is hurting somewhere. I may not be smart enough to always know where, but I'm sure not stupid enough to think that whipping on him is going to make him better. So I go directly to a good horse vet and have him checked over from top to bottom. After appropriate treatment and a few weeks rest, the horse is usually good as new. Barrel racing is harder on horses than most people think."

This is a very different ending from what happens to the sore horse being whipped for not working up to par. At first the horse will become scared and high. The horse does not have any idea why he is being beaten.

Frequently, his rider will rationalize and say that the horse still runs good at home, so he can't be sore. But practice sessions are not the real thing. The tension and excitement that drain energy are missing. Riders usually don't ask for 110% in practice. You must listen to what the horse is telling you now — not what he said yesterday or the day before.

Also, horses usually don't quit wanting to work all at once. They begin to get sore and try a little to avoid competition. No one listens. The next week they are a little more sore and try a little harder not to have to work. Yet

87

All athletes need a warm-up period before they exercise. Here, a pre-race warm-up will help prevent soreness and injury.

the pain is still at a level that can be masked by the adrenaline surge that hits them as they kick into high gear. But without relief or treatment, this won't last for long. Soon the pain will become so great that the horse will run through the bridle, refuse to turn the first barrel, or show other demonstrative behavior which should tell his rider that he has had enough.

What will the horse get for his suffering? More beating, banging, spurring or snatching? How can any horse put up with that and still *want* to perform?

Another problem Merrill brought up was overtraining. A horse ready to show, race or run does not need to practice, practice, practice. She said it was not unusual for barrel racers to ask a horse for four or five practice runs during a training session before a rodeo. Most of the time, this is totally unnecessary and destructive. "Once I get a horse ready and he is doing good, I only run him at the rodeo," Merrill commented. "A speed event horse, just like a race horse, has to be fresh to give his best effort. There are only so many runs a horse can make during his career, so why should I shorten his career by practice running him? There isn't any money put up and overworking one will just make him sore quicker and undermine keeping his mind right."

Mental training and conditioning is sadly neglected for today's equine athletes. Trainers should take notes from sport psychologists as well as sports physiologists. The attitude that an athlete has towards his event can make all the difference between the champion and the "also ran."

Using reward training provides positive results. Punishment does not inspire brilliant performances. The punished athlete will only do as much as he needs to in order to escape the punishment.

A mundane, repetitive training routine creates boredom. Good horses have active, curious minds that respond to the challenge of learning new things. If properly taught, the equine athlete will develop a sense of pride in his ability to perform, but it can be extinguished through boredom or pain. This is how most pleasure horses become ring sour. Spending too many hours a day going around an arena at a slow gait with his mind in the middle and nothing to look at or think about makes a horse sour. It takes a special kind of horse to enjoy being trained like this. Mellow, uncreative horses can take this kind of training without becoming sour. Most young horses and other athletes can't take the routine without developing a poor attitude about being ridden.

Training doesn't need to be like this. Pleasure horses can be ridden out on the trail, taught to sidepass, spin and do other things besides just go slow and steady. A block of time can be created during every training session when a horse will want to work slow and steady. Then the opportunity exists for the behavior to be rewarded. This is better than the opposite choice of forcing the horse to go slow when he is not willing or ready to accept the challenge.

There are all sorts of bitting rigs, martingales and mechanical gizmos that trainers use to force horses into a frame. Used improperly, they build resentment rather than better performance. The horse comes out of the barn dreading the training session rather than lively and curious about what things he and his trainer are going to do. Forced into a set frame and held to a slow gait during the entire session is not the way to build a relationship with an equine partner aimed towards excellence. In fact, it is the fast track to ring sour.

For the fast-moving performance horse, the opposite is true. Too much speed too soon in training will quickly change a horse's attitude. For many horses, acceleration causes fear. It is imperative that a horse be able to handle a task slowly with some precision before being asked to perform it faster. It doesn't matter whether we are talking about race horses, barrel horses, reining horses, or show jumpers: a horse must have a clear perception about how the performance should be done before speed is added. Nor should speed be added all at once, but just a bit at a time, keeping the horse relaxed at each increment.

Speed makes horses high, and they must learn to think at each level before the trainer asks for more speed. If they don't have that chance, the result will be the same: a race horse who throws his head up and runs blindly around the track, a barrel horse who runs down the fence instead of turning the first barrel, a reining horse who scotches during his rundowns and refuses to stop until the rider tears his head off or runs him into a fence, or a jumper who crashes through fences without even trying to jump them.

Speed makes horses high and they must be able to handle each increase before the trainer asks for more. If they don't have that chance, the result can be like this young racehorse: throwing the head and up and running blindly around the track

Obviously, it is better never to let a horse get like this, but what can you do to retrain the ring sour horse? First, follow Merrill's suggestion. Be sure that the horse is sound. If it is not a physical problem, it is time to deal with a mental problem — and retraining a mind can be a lot harder than reconditioning the body.

For the speed horse, you must find a way to eliminate the nervousness. If the tension is from fear, back off and slow down. Do something else with the horse until he gains confidence in you: trail ride, work cattle, or try a new event. Introduce him back to speed one step at a time. Change the location of where you train him. Also, surprise will work on your side. This horse expects certain things to happen; remove his expectations and replace them with new, positive experiences.

Show him barrels out in a field, jog a pattern. Stop, get off and lead him back to the barn. Whatever you come up with, make it different from what he expects. That this works on all kinds of horses is demonstrated in this story told to us by a race horse trainer.

"I claimed a cheap, older horse off of a leading trainer at one of the big Eastern race tracks. This horse was so sour he would rather fight than be taken onto the track to work. So every morning I ponyed the horse around the backside as I checked on other horses and visited with folks. Every ten days I'd enter him in a race. That was the only time he saw the track and he always finished in the money for me."

Merrill O'Neal also told us about one of her ways of getting ring sour barrel horses to run. "The trick is not to let them get high before they work. I'll warm them up real slow by walking and jogging slow circles. I never stop a horse like this hard because it is sure to get him charged up. Should he try to get high on me, I get off and walk him around. I do everything I can to keep him *relaxed*. I like to take a horse like this in the alley and just let him stand there quietly. And, above all, I try and make each barrel run a pleasant experience for all my horses by letting each horse use his own style and rewarding their try."

A horseman in the world of racing once summed up Merrill's comments in another way. "You can teach a horse to do anything that doesn't cause him immediate pain or discomfort." It takes a good horseman to recognize the pain or discomfort, to know how to avoid as much of it as possible, and to get a horse to want to work through the rest of it for you.

CHAPTER 11

All Fall Down

My two-year-old filly really surprised me the other day. We were trail riding with a group of my friends. Stopping within sight of the barn to wait for stragglers, all of a sudden, my filly fell down. I jumped off but the incident really spooked me. I led the filly back to the barn and haven't been on her since

Sally

It was the third day we had saddled the nice looking gray Quarter Horse filly that was in for breaking and evaluation as a cutting horse prospect. As we rode into the big arena from the round pen, the filly was as relaxed and quiet as you could ask any green horse to be. After a few rounds, Jim asked for a trot. At first the filly appeared to show some signs of minor distress, but she quickly settled down and performed the task at hand.

Then, suddenly, the unexpected happened: the young mare buckled at the knees, lay down and refused to get up.

Although confused by her behavior, our first thought was that, *maybe*, the filly had become cinch-bound. This would have been a little unusual at this stage of training, but it was a possibility, especially since some fillies can be unpredictably fragile-minded.

Jim loosened the girth but got no response. The filly refused to move. We knew that we could not tolerate this behavior as it might easily develop into an escape mechanism, one that the young horse might learn to use to avoid any task she deemed unpleasant.

To discourage this, Jim pulled off his chaps and flogged at her a few times. Still, the filly refused to get up.

We then decided on a more tenacious approach because we felt that it was imperative to regain control of the situation. So, to accomplish this, we tied the filly's feet together. It had been her decision to fall down, but it would be our decision when she could get back up.

Almost an hour passed before the young horse decided to try and get up. Of course, she was unable to do so. We let almost another hour pass before we went back to the arena, untied her feet and allowed her to get up. Getting back on, Jim rode her around the pen at a walk and trot. No more problems occurred and we thought that the point had been made.

We were sadly mistaken! The next day was a repeat performance. We were more surprised and confused; this is not a typical behavior pattern of a young horse.

We hesitated to increase the punishment for the filly's action, but couldn't find any physical reason why the youngster was behaving in such a fashion. We called the owner and explained the situation. We quizzed her about any history that might have led to this kind of behavior but there was nothing unusual about the filly's upbringing that would explain her actions.

The third day she exhibited this strange falling down behavior, the reason became clear. After being ridden only six days, for no more than thirty minutes a day and never faster than a trot, the filly bowed both front ten-

dons. Obviously, the unusual behavior was caused by the
filly trying to escape from the pain and stress being
inflicted on her front legs. It has been twenty years since
this happened and we have never seen it happen before or
since in a horse being ridden so lightly but, we now know,
it is possible.

Most horses who use this type of escapist behavior
do not have such a blatant excuse. Still, they do share a
common thread: these horses feel that they are being put
into a situation where they are under intolerable pressure
or stress. These unendurable situations may be caused by
physical pain, mental stress or a combination of both. It
commonly occurs like this:

A rider is determined to teach his young horse a new
task. The new cue fails to cause the desired response.
After scolding the horse for his failure to understand, the
rider repeats the same cue. Again the horse fails to understand. Another reprimand, followed by the same cue . . .
the sequence continues. This situation puts a lot of mental stress on a horse. He can't figure out the cue and
knows that he is going to get in trouble for not knowing
the right response. For some horses, the mental anguish
builds up to the point where they try to escape from the
pressure by lying down.

Or like this:

A young horse is asked to accept the pressure of a
cinch around his heartgirth. While this physical pressure
is a relatively painless restriction, the youngster feels like
he can't breathe; his mental stress increases up to the
point that he can't think. His solution: escape by lying
down.

Horses differ in what it takes to drive them into such
a state. What one horse can handle may drive another
over the edge. Once distressed, individual horses also deal

with discomfort in various ways. In some horses, the reaction to unacceptable levels of stress is violent, angry and aggressive emotions, which they use to rid themselves of the person or object causing the problem. This approach seems reasonable; we might react in a similar way if put into an intolerable situation.

Then there are horses that have the totally opposite reaction. Instead of either trying to fight or escape from their torment, they practice passive resistance. These horses mimic Gandhi's approach to altering the environment: they lie down and refuse to accept any more riding or training.

There are other specific training sequences where this behavior is more likely to occur. A "Gandhi-ized" horse can be stressed during his initial introduction to being mounted. Instead of trying to escape the stress of having a human on his back by violently bucking, rearing or kicking, this horse simply rocks back, leans over and falls down. The rider has no choice but to get off or risk being squished.

When a horse learns he can escape from an unbearable situation simply by lying down, it is inevitable that the behavior will be repeated. Further, when passive resistance allows the horse to escape from the perceived ordeal, the reward has the power to turn the degrading action into a learned response. The horse learns quickly that he has a tool which allows him to escape from uncomfortable situations.

How do you eliminate this rather repulsive and certainly undesirable behavior? The solution that comes most immediately to mind is to make the experience of lying down more unpleasant than whatever it is the horse is trying to escape. This theory is based upon the supposition that a horse will not jump out of the frying pan and into the fire — at least not more than once!

The old-timers' response to dealing with this behavior was to tie the horse up while he was still on the ground. Then, a wagon sheet was thrown over the horse so it was unable to see. To add even more discomfort, the horse could be flogged periodically for several hours. Of course, one did not have to use all of these steps if one or two were sufficient. The key point to drive home to the horse was that lying down on the ground was the last thing in the world that he wanted to do.

Making lying down on the job an extremely uncomfortable thing to do is still the best way to eliminate this potentially dangerous behavior, but if we use our "higher intelligence," we might be able to conjure up more humane techniques. For example, one trainer told us that rather than torment a horse in the old style, he simply carried a canteen of water on the saddle. When the horse lay down, he poured about eight ounces of water in the animal's ear. He said the horse would then get up to shake the water out of his ear. After a few doses of this, the habit was broken.

We have always intended to try this method, but by the time we get the eight ounces of water measured and try to hit the ear cavity, the horse is already up and looking a bit wild-eyed. So, as of this writing, we have not yet gotten any water in an ear but it does sound like a workable idea!

Seriously, dealing harshly with an undesirable behavior is usually traumatic to the horse and does not serve to strengthen the bond between horse and man. It is therefore much better not to let the animal develop such a behavior in the first place. If we see a young horse that is uncertain about the introduction of the binding girth, we introduce tightness in stages, using the technique discussed in detail in Chapter Five on horse phobias.

In the case of the young horse that wants to lie down when heavy weight is placed on his back, one solution is to keep him walking in small circles while the rider is easing onto his back for the first couple of times. A horse is less likely to go down when he is moving forward.

The most important key to handling any of these situations is to recognize the problem before it becomes full blown and to be able to determine *specifically* what is causing the horse to exhibit this escapist behavior.

Armed with this knowledge, we can develop techniques to manipulate the horse through the potentially distasteful situation and still get the job done. When we have to resort to punishment, force or pain to eliminate escape behavior, the horse has created a problem which overcomes our intellect. Frustration often makes us resort to primitive tools. In other words, in these cases the horse is smarter than we are. To regain the upper hand we resort to causing the horse fear and pain.

As horse trainers we should strive to learn from our mistakes, reaching for Nirvana, a place where horses can be trained without fear, force or punishment — a place where man uses his intellect instead of his brawn to manipulate horses into wanting to perform his every wish.

CHAPTER 12

Ties That Bind

Fear gripped the young foal's body as he felt the restraint of being tied up hard and fast to the snubbing post. With his hind end dug in, he threw his weight backward, stretching his neck as his head was bound hard and fast to the post. Unable to break free, adrenaline pumped up his muscles as he fought the rope with all his strength. Finally something gave. There was a sharp pain in his neck as the vertebra dislocated. For the rest of his life, the colt would carry his head held off to one side.

(Jim) *Coming up in the western tradition, when I was in my 20's it was unthinkable that I would own a horse that couldn't stand tied. I knew that there were such horses since I'd heard that eastern horses were not trained in this amenity. This incredible fact was confirmed by the occasional eastern horse that had been shipped west and, invariably, broke his reins and ran off over the hill when tied. Trying to figure out why easterners wouldn't teach this important lesson to their horses, I decided that these horses must have been pampered by wealthy owners who had a groom around to hold the horse for them when it was not being ridden.*

After crossing the Mississippi River and going east to

train budding horsemen and women at the University of Maryland, I realized that it wasn't the odd horse here and there that didn't know how to stand tied. A lot of eastern-trained horses and most Thoroughbred racehorses were and are never taught to stand tied. Since the reasoning behind this practice still escaped me, I was determined that, at least the horses under my care would be educated in this form of equine discipline, a conviction which was to bring about a major mind expansion for me.

I set out to find a horse on which to demonstrate my conviction to my students. Actually, I didn't have to look very far. The University's herd was full of gentle horses that were well trained enough to stand tied as long as the reins were loosely attached to a ring or tie post. Tie one up hard and fast, however, and it was a different story. The horses would go berserk, fighting until something snapped. Still amazed that seasoned riding horses would behave like this, I asked the students to bring me the worst fit thrower they had.

"Oh, no", they said, "You shouldn't use Sea Mist. She's a Thoroughbred to boot and she is bred to fight the restraint. She'll never, never give up or learn to accept that kind of submissive behavior."

Of course, the challenge of an untrainable horse piqued my desire to prove that this cowboy could train any caballo to stand and stay at a designated spot. "Bring her on", I ordered.

As they returned with the big, strapping three-year-old filly, I knew that I could not make the same mistakes that previous trainers had made with this horse. I needed to know the answer to four questions:

Had the filly been tied up using a nylon halter?

Had a lead rope made out of 3/4 inch cotton been used?

100

Did the lead shank have a heavy duty bull snap on it?

Had the filly been tied hard and fast to an immovable object?

The answers to all these questions was not affirmative so we remedied the negatives until the list was complete.

Unfortunately, having new and stronger equipment instead of the more traditional English leather equipment did not solve the problem with this escape artist. Since she had always been able to get loose in the past, she was fully committed to the notion that she could always do it. She broke bull snaps, nylon halters (usually at the buckle) and ropes. When all else failed, she threw herself on the ground and sulked.

Things were not going well for my training demonstration. This 16.2 hand, 1200 pound Thoroughbred was turning the situation into an embarrassing moment for the new man from Texas. This meant escalation — more time and commitment on the part of the trainer. Instead of going about the normal routine with even stronger equipment, the time had come to put a real effort into modifying the behavior of this horse.

I took a 30' 33-strand nylon rope and made a loop around the filly's heart-girth, securing the loop with a bolon knot (which doesn't slip and can be untied after it is pulled down). I took the rest of the rope between her front legs and ran it through the bottom halter rings like a lead rope and tied her to a 30-year-old water oak tree.

I was sure she couldn't break this rig but, boy, did she fight. She rubbed the skin behind her elbows raw as she pulled and skinned up her hocks from squatting and setting back. But she stayed tied. This was Day One.

I left daily instructions with my students to halter the

mare, lead her to the same spot, tie her up and leave her for three hours. After a little over a week, the un-tie-able Thoroughbred filly would no longer take the slack out of the rope — not for any reason. Then it was time to replace the heavy duty gear with a regular halter and lead. At first the filly was tied up in the stall, then the barn and finally outside. Like all good western horses, she was now trained to stand tied.

Looking back at this event, we are reminded of the roots of our current philosophy on retraining "breakers." Today, before we would put a grown horse through this regimen, we would have to be convinced that without this training the horse's usefulness would be greatly diminished. Our dramatic change in thinking has been caused by the realization that older horses run a risk of crippling or killing themselves when forced to deal with this type of submission. While the worse scenario doesn't happen very often, it does occur and the risk of it happening to your horse must be weighed before you decide to undertake this type of retraining.

The best pathway around this problem is to never let it happen in the first place. Foals should learn to stand tied at an early age and they should never learn they can escape. This statement raises the question, " At what age should this type of training be started?"

It has been our experience that foals need to be a certain age before they can most easily learn this lesson. This idea began when we tried teaching a group of 14 early-weaned foals that ranged in age from three to four months to stand tied. Every day the foals were brought into a large corral, caught, and tied to the corral fence for one hour. Over a period of five days, it appeared that the foals retained relatively little of what had happened the day

The old belly band technique has the power to convert many tie breakers — but is it worth the risk?

before. Each day they would begin by fighting the restraint like they expected to escape but, by the end of the hour, they would quit the vigorous attempts to break loose and stand to the tie. The next day brought a repeat of the same type of behavior.

However, when the same technique was used on a group of six to seven month old foals, their behavior was markedly modified each day. It seemed that these foals retained more information about being tied the previous day. Every day they made progressively fewer attempts to escape being tied until, by the fifth day, they would not pull back at all.

By beginning to train a foal to stand tied at a proper age, we can reduce the risk of bodily injury and, in most cases, reduce the time and energy the horse commits to escaping the restraint.

We know that horses have a natural desire to escape

restraint the horse can accept. Then each training session gradually removes more and more freedom in such a way that the horse accepts and does not fear the loss of mobility. By not triggering his "fight or flight" syndrome, training is accomplished on a positive note — a goal that we strive for in all training situations.

CHAPTER 13

Not My Head!

As the hand slid up the side of the neck, his head got higher and higher. The whites of eyes spoke of the fear being triggered by the request to latch the halter behind the ears. The next moment the colt bolted and ran to the side of the pen.

Bootlegger Zan was an unforgettable Quarter horse mare residing at Texas A & M University in the mid-60's. Yet it was not the fact that she was by the great Quarter Horse sire, Zantanon H, or that she was the dam of a Texas State Reining Champion that made her so memorable. It was because all her babies were very difficult to halter break.

It began with our exposure to one of her yearlings, a colt that would react violently if touched around the top of his head. Our first thoughts on the matter centered on a common practice in that part of the country. In those days, it was usual for folks working with young horses to twist or twitch an ear as a means of restraint. We assumed that this particular colt must have had a bad experience when someone eared him down incorrectly. This indiscretion caused him to become headshy.

The following year, Zan's weanling poked holes in

our theory. This baby had the same reaction to being touched about the ears. A close physical examination could not produce any reason for the foal to be overly sensitive.

The third year and the third foal provided the answer. We kept a close watch on this baby, always being present whenever the foal was caught or handled. At no time was the horse eared down or mishandled about his head. When it came time to wean and halterbreak that year's crop, Bootlegger Zan's newest baby showed the same violent reaction to being touched as the previous two foals had shown.

Can it be that certain traits such as ear shyness are inherited? Or would it only appear that way because a trait such as sensitive ears or poor vision predisposes a horse to behave in this manner? In the case of the unforgettable Bootlegger Zan, the answer to either of these questions could be "yes."

Unfortunately, heritability is not usually the culprit causing headshyness in horses. In most instances, head ducking and dodging is a learned behavior caused by poor training techniques that teach the horse to avoid human contact.

A case in point would be the handling of the young male horse. A normal juvenile of the equine species invariably seems to have an oral fixation beyond anything Sigmund Freud could have imagined in humans. This insatiable urge to taste every living thing eventually leads to human flesh. At first, it is easy to overlook a little nuzzle by this friendly male but, too soon, his lips are not the only thing being pressed upon the skin. Love nips with teeth included carry quite a different sensation. Most folks agree it is now time to draw the line.

The accepted modus operandi to correct the behavior

(that has already gone too far) is for owners to slap or swat at the fun-loving youngster whenever he attempts to play "mouthing a human." Yet, unless a strong whack can be delivered every time, this game is destined to turn into a sparring match: the horse nips; the owner swings; the horse ducks. Now the human partner in the herd of two finds himself in the unenviable position of having constantly to fend off the colt's aggressive advances.

Sooner or later, even the most patient owners will get frustrated and realize that they must be tougher. Perhaps, they think, carrying a stick or a bat will allow them to hit their mark and make their horse quit that irritating and potentially dangerous behavior.

Don't bet on it!

A horse trained in this fashion is really good at the game. When the stakes go up, the horse figures he must get better at avoiding the blow. Instead of eliminating the problem, this horse is well on his way to behaving like a punch drunk prize fighter that ducks and dodges any time movement occurs around his head.

This is just one way headshyness can be caused by smacking at a horse's head in the wrong fashion. Striking at the poll of a rearing horse, slugging at a horse who is tossing his head or slapping at one that is refusing to accept a bridle are all good ways to create the problem. So well accepted is this fact that many of the big horse-producing ranches in Texas have a standing rule that horses are not to be hit in front of the shoulder.

Less common and harder to cure than the above examples is self-induced headshyness. This type of behavior is often brought about by a traumatic experience of running into some man-made device such as an electric fence or barbed wire. We have had two horses brought in for training that had caught an ear on an electric fencing wire. From that moment on, neither one would willingly allow a person to touch them about the ear or poll where the shock took place.

Into this category also fall the horses who are head-shy due to a physical injury such as a blind eye or an abscessed tooth. And then there are horses that are ear-shy due to an infestation of ear ticks.

To live with or cure headshyness, it is important to understand which of these reasons is the culprit behind the behavior. If it is ear ticks, a medicated ear spray will eliminate the causative agent, but care should be taken not to produce a horse that turns headshy from being spritzed in the ear.

Again and again, it seems to come back to the same point: be sensible about handling a horse's head. His eyes, ears, nose and lips are sensitive structures that he is compelled to protect. Handle them gently, for it is a lot easier to prevent headshyness than to cure it.

Reschooling the headshy horse can be rough. It may mean a commitment of time, strength, ingenuity and patience. But first you must decide on whether it would be better to use a desensitization technique or a flooding procedure. We have used both successfully.

In one instance, we couldn't put a bridle on the head-shy horse that had been electrically shocked behind the ears. As soon as anything came close to the top of his ears, he went crazy! We felt he needed desensitization.

A length of 1/4 inch sash cord was made into a loop resembling a lariat. Every day, the horse was caught using a big halter that could be fastened down on his neck. A strong lead shank was snapped so the horse could be held relatively still while the desensitization process proceeded: the flipping of the loop over the ears.

We began by making a big loop, one that would not

touch his ears as it was flipped over his head. As soon as the horse accepted this, the loop was drawn tighter so that it just barely touched the tips of his ears during the procedure. Slowly, the size of the loop was decreased until the horse no longer objected to the action. It was then a small step to substitute the bridle for the cord loop and — voila! — the horse no longer objected to being touched around the ear. The entire sequence of events took about a week with many repetitions each day — a short commitment of time to alleviate a problem that could cause a lifetime of distress to both horse and humans.

While desensitization is usually the best choice, occasionally a situation arises when flooding seems to be a better answer. A two-year-old buckskin gelding that was bred and raised on the farm showed a similar tendency to reject being bridled. After checking for ear ticks or other physical roots that might be causing the problem, it was determined that the colt had a bit of a "cauliflower ear." Evidently, the structural design of his ear gave him some discomfort when the ear was bent over to slip on the bridle.

Knowing the problem, it was easy to avoid crimping the ear, but the horse was still super-sensitive and would either raise his head or turn it sideways making it difficult to reach his poll. To eliminate this escapist behavior, it was decided that a flooding technique would be the best course of action.

This meant demobilizing the colt's head so that he was not able to escape advances made towards his sensitive ear. Restraint consisted of tying his head to his front leg. Once convinced that he could not escape, it was easy to prove to him that a gentle human touch would not cause discomfort to the ear he was trying to protect. In three days, the horse was no longer headshy.

Whether the cure to the problem is based on desensitization practices or flooding procedures, success will be based on how the technique is applied. It is important to come in contact with the sensitive area by using a slowly moving hand up the neck. The fingers should be closed, producing a broad surface of touch for the hand. There should be no poking or grabbing. No quick movements! No sneak attacks!

The horse needs to know that contact with his head is coming. If he tries to avoid the touch, the procedure must be repeated over and over until the avoidance behavior disappears. Only then is it time to move on to the next step.

As contact between horse and human becomes more acceptable, the thumb and palm should be used gently to cradle the ear. Tender massaging and rubbing of the ear must be done to get the horse completely desensitized.

Remember, do not use the tips of the fingers or an open hand. No getchi-getchi-goo stuff! A horse is not a human baby nor is he Fido! He evolved with different instincts and reactions to stimuli than predatory species such as man and the dog. Understand your horse's problem, have a reasonable plan based on his natural response, and you can reasonably expect to cure him.

CHAPTER 14

You Stump-Sucker, You!

The beautiful mare was a celebration of equine beauty, gorgeous in every way, a true queen of the horse world. Regal, graceful, refined...until she moved to her stall door, hooked her teeth over the edge, sucked back and made a sound not usually a part of polite company, either equine or human.

Finding a cure for the stump-sucking horse has been as difficult a task as locating the lost city of Atlantis. Stump-sucking, or cribbing as it is called by folks without stumps in their pastures, is an act which begins with the horse hooking his upper incisors on some object, preferably of wood. The horse forces his teeth into the wood by flexing his neck muscles, an exercise which allows him to gulp in air. As the air rushes down his throat, the characteristic sound associated with cribbing can be heard — "Aaaaaa-uph!"

It is a repulsive display from such a majestic animal as the horse, but is it actually harmful? Yes! To begin with, it is safe to say that cribbing is highly injurious to the price of a horse. The intrinsic value of a horse is at least partially determined by his esthetic appeal. Since

The cribber forces his teeth into the wood by flexing his neck muscles, gulping in air with the characteristic sound — "Aaaaaa-uph!"

this vulgar act is not very attractive, in most circles the horse's value is definitely diminished. In fact, many sales companies demand disclosure of any animal inflicted with this vice. Failure allows the new owner to return the horse to the seller.

Aside from this aspect, hooking the teeth on a solid object and bearing down does cause excessive wear of the central upper incisors (front teeth). While cribbing does not seem to impair the horse's ability to graze or eat, it may effect his overall nutritional state.

Horses that swallow air often do not have good appetites and tend to have a higher incidence of colic. This does not mean that every horse that cribs has these infirmities. It means that a cribber has a greater chance of being so inflicted than a "normal" horse. So, even though cribbing may not impair function, the wind-swallowing horse is said to have a vice: an undesirable behavior which may predispose him to be at risk.

How does a horse acquire this obnoxious habit? Who

The tell-tale sign of the confirmed cribber: top teeth worn down to almost nothing.

led this horse astray? Was it peer pressure? Was his mother a bad influence? Did he grow up in the wrong neighborhood? Or was it an inherited family trait?

Although there is not much scientific evidence available to answer any of the preceding questions, many horsemen feel that environment plays a significant role in determining whether or not a horse will acquire this undesirable habit.

As is the case with most stable vices, cribbing is associated with boredom. It is generally accepted that horses do not learn to "suck on stumps" unless they are confined. Yet not all stalled horses are destined to be users of the stump.

It does seem that some horses are more susceptible to picking up the habit than others. This leads us to the theory that perhaps certain dispositions are more easily bored in confinement, such as the hyperactive horse or the "intellectually" creative horse. Without carrying this too far, there is some information available that cribbing is more likely within certain families. However, it is not clear whether the disposition to crib is inherited, or whether horses learn the behavior from family members, especially their mothers.

This last possibility seems to be supportable in fact. Young horses can learn to crib from their mothers. Part of the maturation process requires that foals mimic their dams' behavior. They learn to eat what she eats, drink where she drinks and suck stumps where she cribs.

If you are planning on the purchase of a new horse, how could you tell whether the horse you are about to partner-up with is a stump-sucker unless you happened to catch him in the act? It's easy if you buy a horse through a reputable sale. The catalogue should have in bold type the word CRIBBER on the bottom on the page. And the announcer should declare the horse a cribber upon entering the ring.

However, since the sale ring is a small source for horses, what other red flags are available to alert you to the fact that this animal should be subjected to vice detection?

The universal stop-gap treatment for the cribber is to put a tight strap around the throat latch. When the horse tries to flex his neck muscles, the strap cuts into the neck. If the horse is wearing a strap or if there are indentations on his neck which could have been made by such a devise, be on guard. Do not be gullible enough to think that these signs are caused by thin leather straps that are used as identification collars.

To the educated eye, a confirmed stump sucker is hard to miss. A glance at the neck muscles which are flexed during cribbing are a dead giveaway. Constant exercise of these muscles forms an unusual definition in the muscular conformation of his neck. This neck crease is a tell-tale a sign. To be absolutely sure, check inside his mouth. Look to see if there is excessive wear on those central upper incisors which take all the abuse of sucking on stumps.

For the unfortunate owner of a confirmed cribber, the prospects for curing the habit are bleak. The best that can be hoped for is that the behavior can be extinguished by eliminating the opportunity for it to happen. The easiest and first choice for many horsemen is the use of a leather cribbing strap. Yes, these devises actually do serve to curtail the activity. They require a minimum of care, but it is extremely important to check the strap on a regular basis to be sure it isn't rubbing the neck raw or, even worse, it hasn't been lost somewhere in the pasture. It seems hard to believe that a little leather strap could exert such power over a thousand pound animal but it does.

This fact was confirmed again for us when a strap-wearing mare was delivered to the farm. Put out in a field with a group of contented baby factories, cribbing appeared to be the farthest thing from this mare's mind. Quickly she entered the herd and spent her days grazing on luscious green spring grass. One day, to our surprise, we saw the mare sucking on a post. Examination showed her strap had come off. Surely, we thought, she will get enough of that and return to grazing with the other mares. Not so! This horse was such an addict that she would barely leave the post to go to water. In a week's time, the mare lost nearly one hundred pounds. Finally, we were convinced that she would literally die to crib, and the cribbing strap was repositioned around her neck.

Why would a mare refuse to graze, starving herself to near death, just so she could perform this repulsive habit.? One explanation is that the act causes the body to release endorphins, a self-generated chemical that puts the perpetrator into a mild euphoric state. This mare must have been extremely dependent on this chemical to have been willing to die in order to receive a fix.

Fortunately, many horses are not so addicted. It is quite common to find horses that crib in stalls, but do not crib out in the pasture even without wearing a strap. Then there are cribbers that do not crib in steel or wire pens if there isn't any wood for them to sink their teeth into.

These quirks should cause concern for buyers to beware. Several years ago we bought a broodmare that we had been watching for some time. She never showed any signs of cribbing in her wire and pipe paddock, but as soon as we got her home and turned her out behind wooden fencing — you guessed it — she immediately turned into a stump-sucker. Since we had no intention of building the mare her own personal wire and pipe paddock, we resorted to another possible cure for confirmed cribbers: paint all possible stump-sucking sites with a foul tasting liquid! While this is a viable solution, it does have several inherent problems.

To begin with, it takes gallons of fluid and a lot of time to paint suspect surfaces. And that's not the end of it! The treatment must be continued on a regular basis. In the meantime, the confirmed cribber spends all his spare time looking for missed spots.

Due to the frustration built into solving this problem, some innovative solutions have come forth. Based on the hypothesis that habits might be broken if the act causes significant trauma, some folks developed a shock treatment for their horse. The cribbing site was electrified by wrapping it with electric fencing wire. When the horse put his mouth on it, he received quite jolt. To be sure, the horse never did crib again on that spot, or for that mater, anywhere close to an electric fence. However, it was only a matter of minutes before another "cool" spot was selected as his new favorite stump-sucking post.

If all your attempts to cure this undesirable behavior have been in vain, you might consider having your horse go under the knife. There is a surgical procedure which may eliminate the behavior by severing the nerves and muscles which allow the horse to crib. The operative word here is may. It is estimated that this procedure is completely successful 57% of the time. It reduces, but does not eliminate the habit 31% of the time. And 11% of all operations result in no behavioral change at all.

While not a particularly sensitive operation, the surgery is laborious, taking approximately two hours while the horse must be under general anesthesia. All of these factors must be weighed against the expense of this option. The price tag for this surgery is quite a chuck of change for a solution which is only effective 57% of the time.

The only other "solution" that we have heard about was told by an old gypsy horse trader. Please make note that we have never tried this method, or know anyone who has attempted this technique. This is how it was described and the old fella' seemed to know a lot about the procedure.

Take a metal ring (the kind that used to be in bathtub stoppers) and attach it to a copper wire. Drill a hole in the lead portion of a .45 caliber bullet. Slip the wire through the hole so that the unit looks like a clapper out of a bell. Use a hot eight penny nail to burn a hole in the thin membrane under the horse's tongue which holds the tongue to the floor of the mouth. (Surely there is a better method for this part!). Open the ring to insert it through the hole in the tongue membrane. Close the ring and, supposedly, the horse will forever forget about cribbing and play with the bullet under his tongue.

Barring this last "cure," which may be worse than the disease, all the treatments for cribbing are designed to physically inhibit the act. They do not eliminate the desire. Therefore, it is an easy comparison to equate the stump-sucker with other substance abusers and say that cribbing is a disease which is treated but seldom cured. Just like our national war on drugs, the solution is best found in the prevention of the habit.

What are some possible systems that might eliminate the temptation before the habit raises its ugly head? Start by eliminating boredom. Play a radio in the barn. Use goats and chickens to amuse easily distracted individuals. Keep horses in a more natural environment. Remember, they are grazing animals of the plains. Turn stalled horses out as much as possible. And, finally, it helps to let the horse socialize as much as possible with his own kind — as long as they are not users of the post.

CHAPTER 15

Pre-Heat Syndrome

The moment I entered the barn, I knew the transformation had taken place. The mare pinned her ears at me— the glare in her eyes dared me to try and ride her. Ignoring the ominous greeting, I began to knock the mare off. Her skin crawled under each stroke of the brush. She flinched from every touch of my hand. Girthing the saddle up a big hump appeared in her back — the furies were primed for release.

"He's a mare man!"* Invariably uttered in a condescending tone, this comment was used to describe horsemen who preferred to ride feminine equines. Real men, of course, rode stallions. It would be inconceivable to imagine Napoleon or Ulysses S. Grant astride anything but a fiery charger. Yet, one might have thought that after the Civil War, there would have been a change in this philosophy as the need for military men to ride aggressive stallions onto the battlefield dwindled. But, even as the west was being settled in the late 1800's, and the great trail drives were moving toward the North Star, the same leer was heard with "He's a mare man," because geldings now

* *This chapter is written by Jim; he's the "mare man" of the authors.*

were the preferred gender.

It seems that mares have long been considered most useful for producing male offspring and as ladies' mounts, since ladies supposedlyhave a greater insight into the cyclical nature of a female disposition. With this heritage, it is no wonder that I have been repeatedly asked why I prefer riding mares which are so hard to train when they are in heat. My somewhat flippant answer to this question has always been that I would rather ride a mare who is occasionally in heat than a stallion that is *always* in heat.

Although an oversimplification, the answer actually does justice to the question. Perhaps a less-biased inquisitor would ask "Why do you enjoy training mares with all the problems inherent with the sex?" Then my answer would be more direct: if you can prove to a mare that you can train her when she is in heat, she will give you her heart 365 days out of the year.

Over the years many systems have been devised to try and give "mare men" an edge over the fickle nature of the filly in heat. A story is told about one of the greatest cutting horse mares to ever drop down on a cow, Poco Lena, dam of the great cutting horse stallions Doc O Lena and Dry Doc. For many years, this mare was hauled and shown at the biggest cuttings in the country and was a true champion cutting horse. It was reported that the problems associated with her estrus were solved by putting one hundred copper pennies in her water bucket. This, legend has it, kept her from cycling.

I don't know if this solution really works but, today there are certain hormones available that can regulate or postpone the onset of estrus in the mare. This allows us the luxury of avoiding the behaviors which, supposedly, are detrimental to a mare's performance particularly during events like a race or important horse show.

Is all this hoopla made up by male chauvinistic horsemen to downplay the intrinsic value of the female of the species, or do mares actually have serious problems which limit their performance potential? Reason dictates that we should try to understand what this estrus behavior is all about and why some folks think that it is so undesirable that it must be avoided at all costs.

By definition, estrus is the fertile period of the mare's reproductive cycle when she is willing to accept a stallion. In theory, then, unless unrestrained stallions are running around the area, her biological predisposition should not cause the mare's rider any undue problems. Her normal behavioral signs of estrus, such as frequent urination, vaginal discharge and the contraction of the labia major, other than being distracting and causing some minor grooming problems, are of little consequence.

The training dilemma is focused around the effects that higher estrogen levels have on her psyche which can be expressed as hyper-irritability coupled with an inability to maintain attention on the task at hand. This syndrome may strike an anthropomorphic cord in that the symptoms are remarkably similar to the descriptions given by women stricken with premenstrual syndrome. Like PMS, PHS (preheat syndrome) presents the biggest problem during the period of transition. A mare in her progesterone phase, otherwise known as *diestrus*, is basically tranquil. This is a marked contrast to the short-lived, full-blown estrus behavior when the mare may throw up her tail and position herself in a breeding stance at the beckoning call of an amorous male. The real training challenge comes while a mare is moving from diestrus into estrus.

Like all biological systems, there is a great deal of

variation in the way any given mare will behave during this transition. Some mares, to the unskilled observer, appear never to change at all in their attitude towards people or training. At the other end of the spectrum are those mares that are soobvious in their hormonal changes that you can map their cycles each day as you saddle up simply by understanding their attitude towards the job at hand. These are the mares that are hard to ride and train. To be successful is not easy, but the rewards of the female spirit make the challenge worth the price.

High-strung, short-tempered, and irritable mares need a rider who can handle them in a firm but gentle way. I admit the first time I heard this expression, *firm but gentle*, from old-timers I was totally confused. But the importance of the concept was drilled into me by my elders who believed that until one had mastered *firm but gentle*, he would never be a horse trainer. Still, at this early stage in my education, the statement seemed to be a dichotomy, like turn right and left. How can you be firm but gentle at the same time?

Part of the answer is locked in your concept of time. You can be firm and instantly change to being gentle so that you are being firm and gentle in the same synchronized act. This is an important concept in the control and manipulation of the fractious filly. If you use total dominance by being a constant aggressor, the filly will rebel and fly apart. She will bitch and pitch and fight back against too much firmness. On the flip side, if you are overly sympathetic to her hormonal woes and loosen your dominance and lessen your aggression, the more she will protest by becoming flighty and unwilling to acknowledge your presence. Without the security of *firm but gentle*, the mare will want to do her own thing: that is, to find a group of horses to whom she can squeal and wring her tail.

The key then is to be firm, dominant and aggressive, and yet be able to back off at just the right moment to avoid rebellion and a fight. Remember, timing is everything.

I recently came across the worst case of PHS that I have ever seen, in an extremely well-bred Quarter Horse filly. By a champion stallion and out of a world champion halter mare, the filly went out on the circuit and did very well as a yearling halter horse. Her future looked bright as she was a super mover in addition to having superb halter conformation.

Her world fell apart as she became reproductively active. Her two-year-old year was a disaster. No one could break her. She would train well for a while and then appear to fall totally apart. The more trainers tried to force her to express her former level of training, the more the mare would fight. In fact, at times, it was described as a battle to the death.

After about a year and half of this, the owners called me (since they knew I was a "mare man") and asked if I would be interested in purchasing this incorrigible witch I did and couldn't wait to get her home to try her.

Well, you couldn't have asked for a nicer, more willing filly. She tried to please and worked hard at every task until the day her hormones started to change. What a change! The mare couldn't stand to be touched. Her skin crawled under the grooming brushes and the saddle was hard to cinch down with the big hump in her back. Once on her back, every cue was a declaration of war and she was ready, willing and able to do battle. She expected a fight and when one didn't materialize, she was shocked and taken back.

That was my advantage. Whenever she tried to resist

the cue by bucking or some other imaginative maneuver, I would not allow her to do it because I had her doing something else. When she tried to buck, she ended up spinning. If she tried to run off, she ended up working in small circles.

Punishment was not a part of the session per se. I did not fuss at her for rejecting my cues. Firmly but gently, she was manipulated into doing the cue in spite of what she tried to do. In essence, she lost the battles without even realizing that the rules of war had changed. The old rule that fighting meant that you might either win or lose no longer pertained to training. Now it was a game of strategy, guerrilla warfare, if you will. Strike and retreat before the enemy can retaliate, i.e., to be dominant and aggressive, coupled with firm but gentle. Unable to fight, she had to submit and then it was time to wrap her up.

Hugging, wrapping or framing up a fractious filly is how the goals of a training session are achieved, because fillies always seem to want order and structure to define their existence. To put the filly in a frame, we use all the aids to create a harmony and balance between the rider and the horse — the hand, seat and legs. This should sound very familiar as it is basic to all riding, but it is of particular importance when training the PHS mare. The way that the hyper-irritable mare's body is held in a frame must limit her self-expression to the point that the rider is directing the coordination of movement. Yet the mare can not be smothered so tightly that she will explode or try to escape from the binding aids of the hands, seat or legs. The filly must have just enough freedom that she *desires* control and just enough control so that she feels secure. A hug!

This may not be the most stable of training situations, but it can be one of the more rewarding. I would not be surprised if this discussion didn't conjure up more primordial thoughts such as "why would anyone actually want to ride these crazy fillies?"

Mares bring a uniqueness to the horse and rider relationship. They are biologically herd animals who participate innately in a social order. This gives them the ability to bring into this relationship a desire to please, a desire to belong, and a desire to be a willing participant. You don't have to be a mare man to appreciate these characteristics, but unless you can train a mare every day of her life, she will never completely give you her heart. Once you have had the heart of a filly, stallions and geldings are only second best.

CHAPTER 16

A Match Made In Heaven

I love my horse. She is so sweet and talented. I just have one little problem. Whenever I try to groom her, she tries to bite and kick me.

Selecting the perfect mount is very similar to finding the perfect mate. There are images in our minds of what constitutes perfection. The screening process begins at first glance: hair color, age, eye color, height, weight, facial features and race. In the case of horses, that translates to coat color, height, weight, age, breed and overall beauty.

To bond further, the next step is usually to look for a deeper quality: a personality, a philosophy of life, an inner compatibility — all the things that make it pleasant to know and communicate with this other being. While this is an important part in the development of meaningful human relationships, it seems to receive little attention in the determination of a "first date," or that equally important choice of "first horse."

The consequences of this statement continuously arrive at our farm. Just recently, a young lady with aspirations of being a barrel racer brought in a big, beautiful gray mare to be trained. Although the mare was the kind of horse that any horse person would find a joy to behold, the ambitious rider was frustrated and angry. This filly would rather buck than run a barrel pattern. How could it be that such an athletic equine wouldn't do as she was asked?

The answer was simple. This mare was bred to be a pleasure horse, and although she couldn't read her pedigree, she was well suited to her breeding. The concept of running hard, stopping and turning barrels was not only foreign to her, but downright repulsive.

Making a pleasant union between this horse and the would-be barrel racer was the proverbial task of mixing oil and water. Shake well; the oil and water mix. Leave it alone for a short time, and the oil and water separate again.

For those folks who have experienced this type of disappointment, the beauty of what is inside the horse may take on a special meaning. When someone says, "This horse has a great personality and I know that you two will have a lot in common," don't be suspicious that your "friend" is trying to run an animal at you that looks like a dehorned moose. It may be that you actually are in for a pleasant ride.

Truthfully, as horse trainers, we can say that we've never met a horse we didn't like. Of course, some have been liked better than others, but each horse brings a unique challenge to the trainer/trainee relationship. Yet, these horses are only in our barn until they reach a certain performance level and then they move on. There are a few farm horses that stay here year in and year out. These have to be special individuals which make us feel good every time we feed them, clean their stalls or ride them. They are our friends and neighbors. They give life a special harmony which comes with their companionship.

Knowing when you are looking at such a soulmate is a tricky business. Just as quite a few blind dates and first dates don't turn out to be good experiences, a lot of first encounters in choosing a horse don't work out either. The key in both cases is to gather enough information so you can improve the odds of selecting a winner.

The first facts to put together are the hardest: gather information about yourself. To be objective is difficult for many of us human types. Too often we tend to let our egos get in the way. More often, we claim to be a better horseman than we are. We want what we cannot handle and it falls to the horse to show us the mirror of truth. So, "To thine own self be true" becomes especially important when looking for a horse mate.

If you are intimidated by high-strung, nervous horses, don't try to convince yourself that you want a spirited animal whose energy you will harness for your glorification in handling your phobia. Horses understand little about human phobias, but they do understand weakness and how to exploit it.

In the horse world, there are aggressive, dominant individuals and there are subordinates. If you are in control, you are dominant. If you are not, you are submissive and the horse is in control. If you are intimidated by a thousand pound beast flitting around like a butterfly, you should look for a more stable individual, mellow and laid-back.

On the other hand, if you are a take-charge person, full of energy and enthusiasm for a challenge, this mellowed-out horse will probably be boring. You might be better suited to an energetic horse that will test you in every new situation. Oftentimes, you will find your perfect mate in a young horse who is full of curiosity and that is willing to slide down every vertical bluff, "Snowy River"-style. This type of horse will also have the confidence that, if things get too tough, he is athletic enough to get out of harm's way. Obviously, it is very important that your riding skills complement the horse's abilities or you may be served notice of an impending separation at an untimely and embarrassing moment.

And so the matching goes. Free spirits that don't like boundaries or rules need horses who have a lot of self-confidence. People who are more meticulous are likely to find happiness with horses that want or need someone to tell them where and how to place each foot. This is achieved by the rider developing a detailed set of cues to communicate each movement, a precision ride that definitely limits the horse's freedom of expression. For the horse that likes structure in its life, this type of riding partner is like a marriage made in heaven; to the horse that believes in the God-given right to self-expression, this philosophy would be grounds for a declaration of war.

Another potential battle of antagonists occurs most often in the horse that is insecure and nervous — the Don Knots of Horsedom. To complement this horse, the rider must be able to hold the horse in a frame at all times, a security that prevents his weakness from taking hold. Unfortunately, too often when the equestrian is incapable of this much mental and physical strength, he will try to compensate with undue physical force to keep the animal in check. The coercion excites or frightens the horse and the situation quickly becomes one of gasoline feeding the fire. Too soon, the rider finds himself a candidate for abandonment as the circumstance becomes too hot to handle.

Another volatile match can occur when the member of Equus caballus is sure that he is stronger and more in charge than any individual from the species known as homo sapiens. This horse needs a person that can prove to him that humans *are* the dominant species on earth and that he or she is the unquestionable leader of their herd of two. This mismatch is a very common reason for incompatibility, but for the person who is capable of establishing his worth in the eyes of the horse, the resulting bond can be extraordinary.

But getting there will not be easy! Be sure before you try to bond with this type of horse that you have what it takes to achieve the goal. At the beginning you must be ready for a relationship that seems to be forged in hell. This horse is not naive. He has seen people before, and the contact has proven to him that our species is weak and lacking in the social graces of dominant herd animals. In order for this relationship to flower, it is mandatory for you to prove to the horse that he is mistaken in his deductive reasoning, that he cannot judge all people based on his rather limited exposure to a few.

To change this horse's attitude is usually traumatic, as losing preconceived notions generally are. The person must be willing and able to administer this trauma in order for the union to be consummated. The partner must be confident in the type of coexistence he expects from the horse and he must have the means by which to demand that the horse accept his role. This means administering punishment for improper responses and rewarding desirable behavior.

This sounds like a normal training philosophy, only with this spoiled horse, the severity of the punishment needs to be more committed and intense. Once properly executed, the horse will become dependent on and submissive to his rider. An extremely strong horse and rider bond will develop.

Choosing the equine disposition which best complements your own personality will help you get more out of your relationship with horses. As you begin your quest for your perfect horse, try to be open-minded. If you don't really fit with your horse, sell him. Allow both of you the opportunity to find that special mate.

Don't settle for second best. Think hard and honestly about what kind of horse makes you happy and then go out and find him. Your perfect mount is out there waiting for you. And always remember, color, shape and size won't give you this special oneness. Look deeper.